LAW FOR ONLINE ENTREPRENEURS

A GUIDE TO TOTAL LEGAL AND BRAND PROTECTION

JOANNE FISHER

AND CO.

DISCLAIMER

Now a book from a lawyer would not be complete without a disclaimer and here is no exception. The topics under this area of law are vast. This book is not intended, nor could it ever wish to be, a comprehensive review of every subject area. I have tried to provide you with an overview of the main areas of law that you need to consider when running your online business, not to train you as a lawyer - we are far too complex and boring. I have, however, taken the most significant issues that you may at some point experience and highlighted the main factors for you to consider. This book should never be considered an alternative to seeking independent legal advice and so please, do take advice before actioning anything set out in this book as each and every one of your circumstances and businesses are different and there will never be a one size fits all in this subject area.

———

CONTENTS

DEDICATION

To Eva, Ana, Louie & Oscar - my little bears. Thank you for the gift of being your mum.

And... to you, the entrepreneur that has felt overwhelmed at some point - the game of business isn't an easy one but gaining the knowledge you need to minimise your risk and being brave and consistent will move you further forward than you ever thought possible.

I've got you.

PROLOGUE

A
t eight years old, I made a very conscious decision to become a lawyer. A tiny girl with a very big dream to change the world after LA Law appeared on our screens. Sadly, in my naivety I believed that becoming a lawyer would give me the edge and power to make a real change in the world; little did I know at that age, of the realities of the world we live in. I still believe that every one of us has the power to make an impact; we just need to find our little corner and repeat that message over until there is no one left to listen. In reality, if I'm brutally honest, for a long time what actually happened was that I ended up working for a very large, successful law firm, helping very large, successful companies make very large sums of money.

I got to learn from the best of the best. That's why I was really there, but there was also an air of glamour and excitement like we see on TV. Seeing the number of zeros on some of the deals we were doing was new to me, and it was hard not to get caught up.

It was a fast-paced lifestyle, with high end drinks receptions, pulling all-nighters, and the ongoing pursuit for the next big client win (I could write a whole book on the shenanigans that went on behind the scenes, but that's for another time...) and for a long time, it was where I felt I belonged. But there was always a niggle. I can't explain it fully, but I always knew I was meant to be helping a different group of people. Maybe it was my background - that certainly wasn't the middle- or upper class upbringing that of most of my peers had. In fact, I was the first person in the history of my family to go to university. Perhaps deep down, I never really did feel like I actually belonged in that world.

Now don't get me wrong, I will always love a deal and seeing people succeed, but it's more than that. It's not all about the money or the power. There has to be more to keep us moving forward in the right direction towards our real goals and whether you call that your passion, purpose or mission, it has to be something that hits you really hard, something that makes you want to jump out of bed in the morning and for me, that purpose is to try and break down the stigma attached to the legal profession to make it less elitist and more accessible to everyone. To take the fear out of accessing legal services. To make it less about us, the lawyers, and more about you, the clients. To support the day-to-day people who start a business to find a new way of working that fits their lives and allows them the flexibility and

INTRODUCTION

So now you've heard a little bit about me - thankfully I can say that not every day is as chaotic as that one - welcome to my world!

I am honoured that you are here and ready to take the time to gain the knowledge you need to protect you and your business in the online space.

Whether you are just starting out on your journey as an entrepreneur or are now much further down the line, I can't tell you how proud I am to see you taking this step towards having a totally compliant, fully protected, long-term sustainable business. We're not here playing games... this is the real thing!

I know the legal side of business can feel complicated, maybe even a little intimidating or scary, and to be honest, a lot of the time, boring, but I really want to change that. There is such power behind knowing how to use legal protection to build relationships with your clients and improve not only your business' likelihood of success, but also its value, so I want you to embrace this part of your business.

Expect, at some points in this book, to find some parts complicated. I have tried to keep the details simple and straightforward but if you start to struggle, just stop reading, put the book down and come back to it another day. I am not intending for this book to be something that you read once, never to be looked at again. The intention is that it should stay with you all the way through your business journey, because every business at some point will hit that bump in the road that has legal implications. Then, in those moments when the sh*t is well and truly hitting the fan, or your business is growing and you just need to explore new parts of the process, this book will be there to guide you through. Together, we are going to make legals your comfort blanket. They should inspire you to want to know more. It really is time for the legals to stop being a tick box exercise or even worse, the part of business that people ignore because of fear so really, thank you for being here.

Law is never going to be the most fun or sexy part of your business, but it is an essential part. This bit is non-negotiable. It's not optional when you choose to run a business and you have been playing with fire if that has been you until now. The legal foundations of your business will determine the long-term success of your business, if you win, lose, sink or swim. It is not the part to do when you hit a financial goal, a problem comes your way, or just at some point in the future when you're ready; it is for now.

By working through this part of your business you are sending the right message out there that you really are in this for the long haul, that you take your business, your clients, and your mission seriously. It's a belief in the future of your business, that it's no longer just a hobby or a side hustle that you're hoping the best for. Now this book is not "woo" in any way – it's a practical legal guide that will give you the right foundations for your business and help you navigate your way through your business life with the legal tools, knowledge and advice you need to succeed… but I will be sharing with you some of my beliefs along the way about how setting the right intentions for your business and really owning your power as an Entrepreneur will make all the difference. Mindset is everything and having the right mindset to approach the serious legal side of your business is something to be continually worked on. It may not seem easy in the beginning but stick with it, you deserve the protection.

Without proper legal foundations, in my humble opinion, you don't have a real business - not one that can really stand the test of time anyway. You deserve to build an asset that gives you protection, safety, and options for the future. You're not in business for fun, right? You're here to make a difference, to make an impact, to be taken seriously and of course, to make a profit, so the sooner you start to build on solid long-term foundations, the sooner you will step into your true power as the entrepreneur you are here to be. I have worked with hundreds of entrepreneurs over the last 20 years and not one of them has ever said that this stuff didn't add value... and oh, so much more, so enjoy the process, embrace some of the scary stuff and let's do this together!

CHAPTER 1

WHICH ONE ARE YOU?

Before we go any further, I want to share a story with you; a story of two online entrepreneurs exactly like you, because I see and speak to you every single day. One of the scariest things I hear from business owners before they have done this work is "But why do I need it? I've done ok until now." And it sends a chill down my spine. Ok, that's a bit dramatic, but it does worry me. I'm not here to instill fear in you, that's not my style, but the simple fact is, I have seen the other side - the side when things go wrong - and it happens more than you will ever imagine. I have represented so many clients who have failed to properly implement policies or entered into the "back of the fag packet" deals and it never ends well. Have you ever really thought about the best way to negotiate terms or a contract (and for the purposes of this book, those terms are interchangeable - contracts, T&C's, terms, agreements - they all mean the same thing so don't get bogged down in that detail) it will never be once a relationship has started to break down. Once the rot has set in, trying to reach an agreement that suits everyone is like walking through tar... ask anyone who has ever been divorced. I've been there and I wouldn't want to go there again.

Think about it when you are just about to start work with someone, both of you are open to the potential the relationship is going to bring, so this is the perfect time to be talking about what you are expecting of each other. We will go into much more detail of this later in the book but for now, just let that sink in - you cannot negotiate terms when you are already in dispute – it's just not possible.

Now back to those two entrepreneurs. For the purposes of this book, I have called them Eva and Ana. Now you wouldn't expect this to have been one of the toughest decisions I had to make when writing this book but... it wasn't the easiest. I have worked with many amazing women and every time I came up with a name, I could link it to someone I know or have worked with in this space and because my mind works obviously like a lawyers should, I immediately knew the risks of one of those amazing entrepreneurs becoming offended and wrongly assuming I was referring to them, so to keep it simple I have used my daughter's names. I even started to overthink that, if I'm totally honest, and wondered if it had some deeper meaning about how I perceive their respective personalities so I then flipped the names around once I had made a decision (yes, my brain can be exhausting sometimes) so you can be sure in no uncertain terms that these two entrepreneurs are entirely fictional!

Right on with the story.

Eva has really big dreams.

She's an action taker, passionate, and with the best of intentions, has dreams of building a great business. She can't wait until the time when she can leave her full-time job and live out her dream business and a life where she's working on her own terms every day.

She is really eager to get going, she's wants it all now and has developed a great idea, feels completely "on purpose" and is fuelled with passion.

She can't wait to get out there and just start doing it. What's the wait - right?

She has put out a few posts on social media and has started to gain some traction. People are talking to her, showing interest in her ideas… this might just work!

There are people asking to work with her, and being the action that taker she is, Eva takes action and before she knows it, her sales page is out in the world, she has paying clients into her personal bank account, and she is doing really well within a few months. She has great testimonials and is now ready to leave her full-time job!

She is finally living her dream… or is certainly well on her way….

Now you've met Eva, let me introduce you to Ana.

Ana is also an action taker with an equally strong passion and big dreams for her business.

What Ana does is slightly different. She knows she has some planning to do before she starts a business, so she starts doing some due diligence online.

She is looking at the kind of service that she's going to be offering and seeing what others in the online space are doing.

Ana takes some time to think about the name of her business and her potential product or program names. She goes to the Intellectual Property office and does a search for all of these names.

Finally, she decides on a name that's perfect for her that she knows nobody else is using.

Ana then goes to a lawyer. Now, she doesn't spend a lot of money doing this, she just gets some basic advice on what kind of legal structure she should be trading under - should it be a limited company? Should she be a sole trader? Does she need to set up a business bank account? She talks to them about who her clients and customers will be and works out the type of contract she needs to put in place.

She sets up a business website that is clear and has all the policies and procedures that she is advised to have drawn up. She has a business name she knows she can protect, and she has taken the steps to start the trademark process. She's ready to go.

Of course, it taken her a few months and a little investment before she starts generating any income, but when she does, she has a really solid foundation to start growing her business.

Let's check in on Eva, it's been a few months of everything going great, but she's just opened an email.

It's a very long email, it's complicated and it's full of legal jargon.

It's a letter from a firm of Solicitors saying that she is subject to copyright infringement.

Apparently, and unbeknown to Eva, she has been infringing another business' intellectual property, and they are considering taking legal action against her if she does not provide undertakings and stop using her business name within the set timeframe.

Eva panics for a few days and gets really upset, but it's easier to do nothing, so she ignores the letter. She has bills to pay, so she gets back to helping her clients.

A few weeks later, a letter comes through the door. It's from an ex-client that Eva had a bit of a falling out with - it got quite heated, but then, it had all gone quiet so, she assumed it was all fine. The client has issued a claim online and is pursuing her for breach of contract.

Eva is really happy running her own business and, financially, she is quite successful. She loves working for herself, but right now she is hugely at risk! She's forced to take advice.

Suddenly, she is no longer able to use her brand because it belongs to someone else… to fight it could cost tens of thousands of pounds.

Also, she now has to defend a claim which, without proper agreements to prove she did no wrong, is going to be really tough and again, cost such a lot of money. Because Eva is a sole trader and not a limited company, she's also put her personal assets at risk and could be made bankrupt!

I wonder how Ana is getting on.…

She's building a great business with really strong foundations and loves working on her own terms, but she's started to notice a few other businesses popping up that are very close to her brand and using very similar copy in their marketing. She isn't too worried as she knows she has her trademark protected. She also has IP notices on her website, in all her materials and has included protective clauses in her contracts, telling people that she takes her brand and protecting it seriously, so she knows this won't be a problem she can't solve but still, it needs addressing.

Each time it happens, she sends a gentle message reminding the other business that she takes protection of her brand very seriously; the lawyer she went to see early on gave her some suggested wording that she just uses it when needed. Luckily, she has only ever had to resort to sending out a formal pre action legal letter once or twice.

Ana also receives a claim from an unhappy client. She realises it happens to the best of us so gave this some early thought. She has a clear procedure for dealing with complaints and knows that if the worst ever comes to the worst and she is found to be at fault, she has the protection of her limited company and business insurance.

Both of these entrepreneurs are incredible at what they do. I've worked with many like them and am lucky enough to support them every day. There is something deep inside of all entrepreneurs that drives them to just 'get out there and do it! So, it's not surprising to me that the Eva's of this world often get caught out. Those creative, fast-paced minds just know they have a talent to share with the world but what I can't express to you enough is that there are certain things that we can't avoid when running a business. Legals is one of them!

Whilst being like Eva is such a gift, she's leaving herself exposed to way too much risk and she doesn't need to. She might be making lots of money and getting way ahead of others in her industry faster, but being more like Ana, and taking time to plan and lay really strong foundations will make sure you stay around for much, much longer. It's the classic tale of the hare and the tortoise all over again... slow and steady when it comes to running a business will serve you well. It is a long game and I want to help you make sure you win.

I'm just going to leave these two entrepreneurs with you for now, but we will revisit them in the book, and you may, by now, be recognising yourself in one of these scenarios. I promise you, there is no judgement from me. This is all said with love, and I can honestly tell you that 99% of the entrepreneurs I work with are in fact more like Eva. I am sure we are all guilty of not always going all in when we're not sure what will happen or if we'll be successful. We don't want to spend money on legals and trademarks when money is tight at the beginning and we are not sure if our ideas will work out, but what's the alternative? It goes right and then you lose it all because a legal issue trips you up?

CHAPTER 2

WHERE DO I START?

CHOOSING THE RIGHT BUSINESS LEGAL STRUCTURE.

S o here goes… let's get started. Remember, I have totally got you so there is no need to get overwhelmed by any of this. Yes, it may feel a little technical now and again, but that's ok, right? Running a business which is sustainable and long-term, with solid foundations that you can safely build upon is going to have moments where it feels bigger than you - that's just a fact we can't shy away from, sometimes business will feel like a struggle for us all but moving through those things in a strategic and calm way will be totally worth it.

Starting a business can feel like climbing a mountain. At the beginning, there are a hundred things that you have to think about from branding, sales, marketing, right through to finance and legals, the list is endless and sometimes can feel like nothing more than an uphill struggle. The very first thing I really want you to be thinking about and asking yourself though, is what level of risk are you willing to be exposed to? Because how you run your business day-to-day will determine the level of risk you are up against and what I mean by that is whether or not you are willing to have personal responsibility and liability for your business debts? Let that sink in for a second.

There are four main types of business structure (there are also subcategories but for the purpose of what you need to know here, I will stick to the most common options). At the end of this chapter, I will also give you a brief overview of the various charitable structures that you can have but for now, we are going to focus on pure profit generating business options. That way, you will know all the different options and really be able to get a feel for which one would work for you and your business.

The main options are - Sole Trader, Partnership, Limited Company and Limited Liability Partnership. Sole Traders and Partnership structures are also referred to as unincorporated and limited companies and limited liability partnerships are referred to as incorporated. These two different ways of operating, i.e., either in your own name (unincorporated) or with a separate legal entity (incorporated), are essentially the ways in which every business will operate and the structure you choose has to be right for you. To be able to make the decision that's right for you however, you first have to understand the risks and benefits of each.

FYI it will never be ok to choose an option because that's what Karen on the internet does!

A big proportion, and I would go as far as saying most entrepreneurs that I am lucky enough to speak to, start their experience in business as sole traders. This is also backed up by government statistics. Let's think back to Eva in the last chapter - she went all in and just hit the ground running, she wanted to get her business off the ground with the least amount of fuss and little or no bureaucracy. She was a sole trader and there are huge benefits of operating in this way if it's right for you and you are aware of the risks. Your finances stay private, anything left after tax is paid is automatically yours, you will personally own all of your business assets and you are not accountable to anyone. But, as with everything in life, there are also some drawbacks to operating in this way. The main one being you are personally liable for all of the business debts. This includes business finance, suppliers, office costs, client, or customer refunds - you name it, you're responsible for it. And if you cannot afford to pay, then your personal assets, including your home, car, savings, inheritance etc. are all also at risk and may be repossessed to sell and pay off your debts. If, of course, you do not have any assets, then you are less at risk, but then you may be subject to bankruptcy proceedings because you would be deemed unable to pay your debts and this can then seriously impede your future ability to raise finance which in turn, could cause problems with you continuing to run your business... so do think carefully and weigh up your individual circumstances when you go down this route.

A similar situation arises with a partnership however, with a partnership, the liability becomes joint. Or more particularly, joint and several in most circumstances - now you might think on the face of it that seems like a good thing, however joint and several means that both parties are 100% liable for 100% of the debts meaning if one party has an inability to pay, the other still has to pay 100% of the debt back if required to do so. You won't automatically have (and where there are more than two partners in their respective shares) 50% liability and while that is the hope, in reality, when things go wrong, decisions that benefit everyone are much more difficult to achieve. Also with a partnership, each partner has to continue to pay the personal tax on their respective profits - the partnership does not have responsibility for that so much in the same way as a sole trader, the liability is personal even though on the face of it, it would appear to be shared. Of course, a huge benefit of being in a Partnership is that there is another person to bounce ideas off and more than one investor in those early business days when a cash injection is likely to be needed.

All in all, setting up your business as a sole trader or partnership is simple and other than notifying HMRC for the purposes of paying your self assessment tax, there are no formal requirements before you can start trading.

Best practice, although not a legal requirement with a partnership, would always be to have a contract drawn up between you to make sure each other's expectations are being met. In law, this is called a Partnership Agreement and a lawyer would be the best person to draft this for you to make sure you are properly protecting yourself and your partner. Some of the provisions that they will want you to include in that document will be how profits and payments are to be dealt with, what happens if you reach a deadlock when making a decision (this means one of you vote in favour and the other against), who will have the casting vote if you can't agree, to avoid the business stagnating, what happens if a partner gets sick, dies or just simply wants to leave the business, a process for handling disputes, returns, buyout. With all of these provisions and eventualities being covered off in a properly drafted agreement, your partnership stands a much better chance of success because nothing is being left to chance.

Now let's take a look at the incorporated options.

As I mentioned earlier, there are two main options - a private company limited by shares and a limited liability partnership. There are also public companies but for the purposes of this book, I will not go into detail on those as most startups will be and will remain a private company limited by shares. A public company is not permitted to offer shares to the general public.

Limited companies are a widely used vehicle to protect a private individuals' personal assets when operating a business. In law, they are referred to as having a "separate legal personality", being separate from that of its owners or shareholders. And this is the beauty of the limited company and is usually why people are attracted to operating their business under this option.

———

But how does it work in practice, day-to-day?

The main point to consider here is that you are separate from your company. You will become the director and shareholder and while you will have responsibilities to always act in the best interests of the company, you are not the business. This distinction between a limited company and being a sole trader is probably where the most issues arise in that people do not understand the concept properly and think of themselves and the company as one and the same, which can have severe consequences.

As we have touched upon, the liability you have when operating a limited company is much more limited, in fact, your only risk in terms of financial exposure is the amount you invest into your business when you become a shareholder. In general terms, when you set up a new limited company and you agree, for instance, to buy a nominal share for £1 your liability is just that, £1. All other business debts, unlike with sole traders, remain with the company and you do not become personally liable for those. There is a caveat to this rule, but that will only apply when you have acted outside of your duties as a director and there is potential wrongdoing i.e., if you misbehave as a director, but on the whole, you will not have to worry about that, so, provided you are doing everything you should do as a director and are not acting dishonestly, I don't feel it necessary to go into detail on for the purposes of this book, but if you are ever unsure, just take advice.

For these reasons, you can see why a limited company becomes so appealing. It ring-fences your risk and provides a wall between you and the general public.

I hope I haven't lost you yet!!

Let's now look in a little bit more detail at how the limited company is owned. I have already mentioned shares and the owners of a limited company will also be known as its shareholders. The value of those shares will change over the lifetime of the business as its turnover increases or decreases. Being a shareholder gives you certain rights in the decision making of the business, known as voting rights, a right to receive a share in the profits of the company referred to as dividends, and also a right to be repaid your original investment as a minimum (or the current value) if the business is closed or possibly sold on. Being a shareholder doesn't however guarantee you management of the day-to-day running of the business as this lies with the director or directors (sometimes referred to as a board of directors). The likelihood is, if you are setting up a limited company that you will become both a director and a shareholder and this is more commonly referred to as an 'owner managed business', but it is worth noting that sometimes, as your business grows, the directors and the shareholders may not always be one and the same.

The administration of a limited company, as you might have guessed, is more complicated than when you are operating as a sole trader, and this is what puts a lot of new entrepreneurs off. Don't let that be you though, without knowing all the facts.

A company is set up through the register of companies and in the UK, this is known as Companies House and is actually based in the city that I am sat writing from - Cardiff in South Wales. This government agency stipulates a number of matters that a director of a company must inform them about, which essentially includes any changes in the constitution of the company (its rules), ownership and management. Therefore, if a director changes, or a new shareholder is brought in, they want to know about it. A director will also have an obligation to file company accounts or financial statements to Companies House each year by a certain date or the company may be subject to a fine.

Due to the fact that the company is a separate legal entity to that of its owner's, taxation is also handled differently, and a company will pay corporation tax on its profits as opposed to an individual paying income tax. This is where the biggest kickback comes when entrepreneurs are deciding on which structure to operate under, and this is because of the perceived double taxation rule. When you are a limited company, there is a second tax to pay as you, as the owner/manager, are also taxed on the dividends you take out from the business. It's this double taxation that often stands in the way of people deciding to protect their personal liability through operating under a limited company.

Whereas the limited company has been with us since Queen Victoria was in reign, the Limited Liability Partnership is a much newer concept and in fact only showed up in the UK in the year 2000. It was around in America for a little while longer but on the whole, this structure has only been in existence in the last 40 years. The main feature of a limited liability partnership is again that limited liability is granted to its partners much the same as with a limited company, however, with a limited liability partnership, you become a member of the partnership as opposed to becoming a shareholder in a company.

Now, you're probably thinking why... why would you need this option if essentially it does the same thing as a limited company, and you would be right to question that. Often things are far too overcomplicated when it comes to the law, but the limited liability partnership is almost a hybrid between the two options and is therefore worth considering. While on the outside, it has all the hallmarks and protections of a limited company, internally it is run more along the lines of a traditional partnership and the members, unlike with the shareholders, are free to run the business day-to-day. In terms of liability, with a limited liability partnership the personal liability will be linked to the amount you agree to be liable for, or the amount you initially invest.

———

So how do you decide which option is best for you?

Taking advice early on is the single most important action you can take. For me, a limited company will always be the better option, but you have to feel comfortable with your decision. This book will do a lot of the groundwork for you, but nothing beats a conversation with an accountant or a lawyer who can advise on your individual circumstances.

When you are looking at the various options, you have to make sure you weigh up all the facts. Remember that as a sole trader, you are entering into contracts personally with your clients, so every time you engage in a transaction with a consumer or another business owner, you are entering into a legally binding contract in your personal name, even if you have a different trading name.

What comes with that is obviously risk if something goes wrong. The level of that risk will be dependent on a lot of factors, such as how much you owe, if you have insurance cover, if you can afford to pay your debts… but worst-case scenario is that your personal assets and your personal solvency could be at risk. The benefit of the less formal structure as a sole trader is that you do get to keep all the profits after tax. Once you've set up the business, you pay your outgoings, you pay your tax and anything that's left after that is yours to keep.

As we talked about above, the limited company is slightly different. In this structure, you have the benefit of what's referred to in law as the corporate veil. If you imagine a sheer veil draped in between you and your business, you are behind it making decisions and being protected. It shields you from exposure to risk and the company is said to have its own legal personality. As such, it can be sued in its own name so you don't have any personal risk, save for that small caveat of if you misbehave as a director, but on the whole, and providing your acting with integrity and taking your role as an entrepreneur seriously, you will not have to worry about that. Provided you're doing everything you should do as a director, a limited company is a safe and sensible choice to make.

The other beauty of an incorporated structure is that if you decide you want to leave the company, you don't necessarily have to close it down. A clean break is much easier to achieve if you want to walk away from it, especially if there are other people in the business. The same applies if you want to sell the business - it's much cleaner as a seller if you're a limited company, because when you are a sole trader, you become the business because you're one and the same, therefore it is much less appealing to a buyer. It's not impossible to walk away but the deal is more complex, and we would be looking to sell on the assets of the business as opposed to the business as a whole, the problem with that being that a buyer will mostly want the liabilities such a debt and potential claims to remain with you. When selling a limited company, you can sell the whole thing. You are protected and you can walk away with less risk of issues cropping up in the future. Again, there will always be a caveat against that for bad behaviour and potential indemnities you may be required to give, but overall, this is generally the case.

One final point before I conclude and one that will be useful when considering which option will suit your way of trading, relates to if you intend to raise finance. You would be led to believe that being a limited company would offer more structure and therefore instill more confidence into a lender, however this isn't always the case, and if personal liability is a determining factor for you when making this decision consider that even as a limited company, if you want to raise finance it is highly likely that your lender will also ask you for a personal guarantee. If this is not a concept you are familiar with, in the most basic terms, the guarantee will effectively put you back on the hook personally for the business debt in the event that the company is unable to pay. So, while the corporate veil is doing its best to shield you, savvy and, some would say, sensible lenders will in most situations, insist that you also sign a personal contract to guarantee payment of the debt.

The opposite is in fact in true of investors, who in general terms, will want to benefit from the limited company or other incorporated structure so that they can acquire a degree of control of your business, subject to negotiation of terms. For an investor, a sole trader business is not usually deemed a viable investment because of the risk it can pose and that combined with the potential tax incentives make the limited company more of an appealing option to them.

So, there we have it. I do hope you are still awake. The trading structure you choose should essentially come down to three main considerations - personal liability, tax and raising finance. While the administration of an incorporated structure is definitely heavier, the benefits that come from the limited liability seem to offer more flexibility and security in the long term, so do choose wisely and always take advice from those who understand your particular business model and the outcomes you are aiming for.

At the beginning of this chapter, I also promised you a brief overview of the various charitable structures that are now have available if you choose to run a not-for-profit organisation. The charity sector has certainly improved over the last few years, with more options now available than ever before so this is an attractive sector for the philanthropic entrepreneurs among us.

In the main there are four options:

- Charitable company limited by guarantee
- Trust
- Charitable unincorporated association
- Charitable Incorporated Organisation (CIO)

The charity structure you operate under will largely depend on what you have told the charity commission you are doing and the activities you intend to undertake, but here's a brief overview of the differences to give you a basic understanding of the different options.

A charitable company limited by guarantee is probably one of the most common. Much like a traditional limited company, it is incorporated and registered at Companies House. Under this structure, the trustees of the company have to submit filings to both Companies House and to the Charity Commission, therefore the duties of trustees in the company are generally more onerous than with a traditional company structure which is something to consider.

A trust is a simpler option and is not as expensive to set up because there is less bureaucracy but there is a potential for personal liability. The governing document of a trust is called a trust deed and each trustee agrees to be contractually bound to its terms by signing up to it. There is no set statutory framework when operating in this way so it largely depends on what the trustees agree which can be appealing.

A charitable unincorporated association, as the name would suggest, is an unincorporated structure that again, is more simplistic in its operation. Similar to a trust, it does not benefit from limited liability and is not a legal entity in its own right, therefore the members are somewhat exposed to risk through personal liability.

The charitable incorporated organisation is the newest form of charitable structure. The Charity Commission have suggested a prescribed form of constitution for the CIO; therefore, it is not as flexible in its approach as for instance the incorporated association, but its members will have limited liability.

Operating under a charity structure is not something to take lightly. One of the key considerations will be the "objects" of the charity meaning what is the philanthropic purpose.

The main premise of a charity is of course that it is not run for profit, the purpose must be greater than that and one of the tests applied when becoming registered is whether or not the purpose or object is in the wider public's interest.

The charity commission monitor trustees closely and issue guidance that will serve you well to understand if you venture down this route. You would be ill advised to take the duties of a trustee lightly and managing risk has always been something that needs a fine balance. Under the Charity Commission guidance "CC3: The Essential Trustee" the following provides an indication of how they expect risk to be handled within a charity structure;

"You and your co-trustees should manage risk responsibly. You have a duty to avoid exposing your charity to undue risk. This doesn't mean being risk averse. Risk management is the process of identifying and assessing risks and deciding how to deal with them."

To a certain extent this ability to manage risk is the same when it comes to running any business be that for profit or not but with a charity as the funds aren't for private purposes the duty and obligation is a more sensitive topic so always be cautious and take early advice.

Whatever structure you decide to operate under it has to fit your individual needs and take into consideration the long-term goals for your business, what won't change irrespective of your choice, is the need to be in control of your business administration. Good record keeping and diligence especially when it comes to handling financial matters will be your best friend. As entrepreneurs the finer detail isn't the sexy stuff, if you recognise that this is where you are not strongest don't beat yourself up, take action and outsource whatever you can rather than fall behind which is an unnecessary stress. You know where your strengths lie and don't be afraid to optimise those and ask for help for anything else - it will be one of the best decisions as an entrepreneur you can make. Asking for and receiving help will never be a weakness.

CHAPTER 3

STOP THE COPYCATS

BUILDING YOUR BRAND AND PROTECTING YOUR ASSETS

I t all starts with an idea. As entrepreneurs, we are so great at this part of running a business – it's why we get out of bed in the morning. We're ready for the next big thing and most days, the ideas just flow. The entrepreneurial brain is fascinating, its ability and resilience to move on to the next idea is one of the most endearing and exciting things about us but, to put it simply, sometimes we just need to slow down.

I get it, the ideas never stop, but in that excitement and passion we can hugely underestimate the importance of protecting the ideas we have or identifying the ones that are worth the extra care and attention.

Picking the right name for your business, programme, service, or product is one of the most important decisions you will make. It's fundamental and can determine the success or failure of your business. It's how we attract the right clients and customers. It's our brand, it communicates our brand values and it's how we build trust with our audience. It's our magnet.

But let's break it down, how much do you value your ideas and creations? I'm assuming, if you're reading this book, that business is not just a hobby to you - you know what you have to offer is brilliant. Yes, some days your mindset may make you think otherwise but you wouldn't be doing this if you didn't think you were worth the risk (a calculated risk anyway!) and just like anything else in our lives that we value, we should want to protect it. We wouldn't let someone walk off with the keys to our home or car or even worse, one of our children, so why do we see the creations of our mind, our brilliant minds, as not being deserving of protection. It's a rookie mistake and you are just doing yourself a disservice if you don't do this properly. You and your business will always deserve protection.

There are some really common mistakes that I see entrepreneurs making when it comes to protecting their brand and I will bet that you will have done at least one, if not both. I've said it before, there is no judgement from me, it's just time to do things the right way.

Those mistakes are either choosing names that infringe on someone else's intellectual property or running with a name that it is just impossible to protect. A little bit of planning and easing a little off the breaks before you put something out there, can make a world of difference in the longevity of your business and avoid wasted time and money. There are some really simple things that you can do to make sure that you have the right name and that it is capable of registration to give you the best protection.

First, let's think about what intellectual property you actually have in your business. You would be surprised at how many business owners don't recognise the extent of the intellectual property assets they hold in their business.

A good starting point is to understand that in fact, it's not your idea that is protected or acquires intellectual property rights, it is the way that your ideas are expressed or articulated. What the hell does that mean, I hear you say? Well, to put it simply, intellectual property rights do not come into existence until you do something with those ideas; when you start writing them down, they become protected, when you record videos, they become protected, when you record audio, it becomes protected... it's what you do with it that counts.

Intellectual property is a key element of your online business, and it should form an integral part of your brand strategy. If you are able to properly understand its value to you and your business, it will undoubtedly give you a stronger chance at growing a market share and becoming the go-to person in your industry which, in turn, increases the value of your brand. Sadly, what often happens is that entrepreneurs only start thinking about protecting their intellectual property after they have started to become successful and that can often be too late. "Why?" you're probably thinking. Well, because not everyone has the same levels of integrity as you and it's not until you start to gain traction in your business that copying becomes an issue - no one copies those just starting out!

Also, what if you have to make changes to your brand because you are infringing on someone else's rights? Do you really want to be doing that once your clients and potential clients have started to associate you brand with what you do?

Before you decide on a name there are searches that you need to be doing to make sure the name you want is yours for the taking and leaving this too late in your business can be devastating, both emotionally and financially.

The other thing we often do not think about with brand protection until it's too late is what happens if your business is going really well, and a buyer approaches you? I can hear you right now in your heads saying to yourself that you're not in this game to sell, that your business is you and no one would ever want it, but I can assure you that if the right offer came along, you would give it some proper thought, because you are an entrepreneur. One of the first questions a potential buyer will ask is if you have secured the intellectual property rights in your business and if you haven't, you can be more than sure that the valuation they are making on your business and its future potential will be hugely reduced or worse, you could lose the sale.

So don't let that be you! Over the next few pages, I will guide you through the different types of intellectual property in your business, how you can protect it and what to do if someone infringes your rights. But let's start at the beginning.

———

So, what is Intellectual Property?

Intellectual Property is everything in your business that you can't physically hold onto and by its very nature, will be protected in one of two ways, either through you not telling anyone about it, which of course will be impossible if you want a profitable business, or because you have made a record of it.

If you consider a traditional bricks and mortar business, their assets are much more easily identifiable, their assets are often tangible items such as stock, products, vehicles, or property among other things. For an online business especially those that are service based the assets are much less obvious and the value lies in the creations of the business owners mind - that becomes their Intellectual Property. It's not tangible, you can't physically touch it, but it's still there - an intangible asset. As the creator of that Intellectual Property, you have the right to prevent others from using it as you would with any physical asset and even more importantly, the exclusive right to its commercial use.

I have come across a lot of entrepreneurs who have not given this part of their business the time and attention it deserves but if I had to choose one thing to tell you, you must do, it would be to properly consider the value and protection of your intellectual property – actually, I would want to tell you a million things but for the purposes of this chapter intellectual property is the beginning, the middle and the end. I understand it can sometimes feel complicated but to get it wrong is not just expensive but also upsetting and in reality, can be the difference between the success or absolute failure for your business.

Let's take a look at the different types of Intellectual Property rights you can have.

So just to be clear Intellectual Property is everything in your business that you can't physically hold onto. It's the intangibles, the assets that you create with your mind, and it makes up the different moving parts of your business. It's the ideas that flow from you, the systems you create, the copy you write, the videos you record... it's all of it and more and it's the key to the value of your online business. This is the gold.

It can be both registered or unregistered. Not all Intellectual Property needs you to "take action" to protect it.

Let's ease in gently and take a look at the more straightforward rights first;

Copyright

Copyright by its very definition is the "right to copy" and it is a body of legal rights that gives the creator of those works the exclusive right of ownership, usually for a limited amount of time. Copyright extends to books, movies, images, songs, video, and written content. Copyright is instantaneous and once a piece of work has been created, it is automatically protected and can therefore only be copied with permission of the owner. There's a common misconception that I am sure you have heard people saying - that they "need to register their copyright". The truth is that's just not the case. Those rights are created automatically so if you see someone using your works without your permission, then you can and should raise it with them. Of course, this is law and there will always be a caveat that applies but I can tell you that more often than not when someone is stealing your copy without your permission, it's not ok and you have the right to take infringement action against them.

Copyright lasts for the lifetime of the creator plus 70 years after, at which point it expires and then it is open to use by anyone.

There are limited circumstances where a defence to an act of copyright infringement will apply but these are only in very limited and specific situations, and the infringer would have to prove their defence applies. It would be extremely difficult for another business owner to claim one of these exclusions when they are simply taking your copy to make commercial gain.

———

So, when can someone use my copy?

There is a concept known as fair use (for my American friends) or fair dealing (here in the UK) which is where an exception to copyright infringement can be relied on when using another person's copy, but as I said it will only apply in limited circumstances, such as when your work is being critiqued or commented on, for news reporting, when its being taught for educational purposes and when its being used and cited in research. It is a concept which is covered by legislation and if someone can successfully claim the defence of fair dealing, then they will not be liable (guilty) of copyright infringement. This is not a defence that you can use when you have taken copy and used if for commercial purposes, for instance, when you are trying to make a profit. It is worth noting however, that if fair dealing is established, it will be a complete defence to a claim of infringement and you should therefore consider this before taking action against another person or business as there may be cost implications if you are unsuccessful. What I mean by that is that you could find yourself paying for both yours and the alleged infringers legal costs - a big no!

When deciding if fair dealing applies, the courts will look on a case-by-case basis, so there's no hard and fast rule here that

I can tell you that will make sure you do not fall foul of this, but if you find yourself in this situation, ask yourself what an honest and fair person would do in these circumstances. If the answer is anything other than the action you're about to take, stop and honestly consider that you might be guilty of infringement. This applies both ways of course, so if someone is also using your material - ask yourself do they have a point - is it a fair use or are they seeking to make a financial gain from your work? If the answer is to make a profit, then my view is that you should always take action to put a stop to it.

To give you a bit more insight into this concept, the best thing I can do is give you some examples of what the courts have actually said; what they tend to look at is if the work claiming "fair dealing" as a defence or justification will affect the market for your original work? "So, what does that mean?" I hear you say – basically, if another piece of work could potentially replace your original work or become a substitute for it and as a result, cause you to lose income because of that, then it is unlikely to be fair.

Another factor they consider is whether the amount of the work they have taken or borrowed from you would be "reasonable" and "appropriate". Now, I am sure you have heard the concept of reasonableness talked about many times. I can tell you, it is the bane of most lawyers lives because of course, this is entirely objective and dependent on the individual circumstances of each particular case, so how can this be a useful concept, right? Well, that's exactly the point; what one person does will not always apply to another, so if you suspect this is happening to you or you may be breaching these rules, my best advice would be to get a lawyer's advice and take the factors I have mentioned into consideration - in reality taking a few paragraphs is unlikely to result in weighty infringement action however, it depends what's in those few paragraphs and what the likely outcome will be.

———

"So, what about Design Rights?" I hear you ask

Design rights protect the appearance look and design of your products. They can relate to the whole or just part and the design can be either 2 dimensional or 3 dimensional. They cover elements of design such as shape colour, texture, material and how a product is decorated, or "ornamented", to use the phrase the Intellectual Property Office use. Much like copyright, design rights are protected automatically however, there is an added level of protection with design rights that you can opt to take by registering them with the Intellectual Property Office. I will discuss this a little later.

When design rights are unregistered however, the same principles apply as with copyright - that you're automatically protected when you create a design without having to pay a fee or register the design anywhere. However, the length of time you are protected for will vary if you choose to register and unregistered rights only protect 3 dimensional products. The best way to explain this would be when a designer creates a drawing before the product comes to life: to be able to protect the drawing itself, a person would have to rely on copyright or register the design, whereas when that image becomes 3 dimensional, it is then protected automatically as a design right and protection will last automatically for a period of 15 years from the creation of the design or 10 years from the first sale, whichever is less.

So, providing your design meets the following criteria, which is the criteria specified by the Intellectual Property Office, then you will acquire unregistered design rights automatically:

- It's an original design – one that's all your own work, and;
- It's a design that's non-commonplace – not widely acknowledged within groups of comparable products

———

But when should you take action and get your design rights registered?

As I mentioned earlier, some intellectual property rights are capable of and require protection by formal registration and these generally fall into three categories: registered designs, trademarks, and patents.

So, let's start with Registered Designs.

The aim of a design right, whether its registered or unregistered, as I mentioned above, is to protect a products appearance. A registered design however protects the complete appearance of the product; including its lines, contours, colours, materials, texture, and shape, therefore, when your business relies heavily on your designs, registration will always be a preferred option - not to mention that it is much easier to prove infringements when a right is registered than unregistered and building a portfolio of registered intellectual property assets will add value to your business.

To register a design right, you have to make an application to the Intellectual Property Office and your application can include up to 10 slight variations of the design in a series. The cost of those are around £50 per design, so the application will require some investment.

Once registered however, you will secure exclusive rights to the ownership of your design, meaning that that no one else will be able to create the "thing" you have designed without your permission. Your registration will override the rights of anyone else who creates the "thing" you have protected, and you will have a right to take infringement action against them to prevent their continued production of it. In legal terms, this is referred to as you having "monopoly" over the design, whereas with an unregistered right holder, there is no monopoly over other similar designs, and it will come down to the facts and evidence of each individual case.

A registered design is much more likely to act as a deterrent to copying simply because there is no onus on a registered design right holder to have to prove infringement.

As your business grows, having a registered right, as I touched on above, will give you options to sell on or license to others.

To qualify a design for registration, you need to meet the following criteria which has been set by the Intellectual Property Office, so always check on these before you go ahead with your application:

- The design must be new
- The design cannot be offensive (it cannot feature graphic imagery or words)
- It cannot utilise protected flags and emblems (e.g., the Royal Crown or the Olympic rings)
- It cannot be an invention

So, provided you tick all the above, you are ready to submit your application, which will give you 25 years of protection for your design, subject to applying for renewal every five years.

Now the one I get asked the most about and the one I am sure you have already considered for your online business…

Trademarks.

This is a big one. It's so important to your brand and protecting its future that I wish I could sit with each and every one of you and guide you through it. You really do owe it to your business to give this more than just a little thought.

What I hear time and time again, is that trademarking is easy, anyone can do it… and that, to be honest, is absolutely right - if you know what you're doing! As I have said before, you do not need a lawyer to do all of this stuff for you but knowing when to take advice is a skill to be mastered as an entrepreneur and nothing is more true than with this topic.

As I spoke about at the beginning of this chapter, the two main issues we see time and time again with business owners when it comes to protecting their brand, is that they choose a name or marketing slogan that infringes someone else's trademark, or they choose something that is simply incapable of protection. Either way, it can be critical to your business.

Time and money wasted and still no trademark. Now, I'm going to be honest, even with all the due diligence in the world, you could still find yourself in that situation, but fore-warned is forearmed and minimising risk is just everything when you are running a business.

———

But what is a Trademark?

Now you might be a little bit surprised to hear this, but Trademarks can be both registered and unregistered. I am not going to go into detail on the unregistered rights that attach to trademarks as in my opinion, it's a rookie error not to take the action and complete registration. Unregistered Trademarks are much more difficult to enforce if someone infringes, but you might have action under the rule in "Passing off", so if you ever find yourself in a situation where your Trademark is not yet registered, do take advice as it may be that all is not lost. A good tip to remember is that you can always use the TM mark against anything that you intend or believe to be a trademark of your business. Best practice will always however be to register with the Intellectual Property Office as early as possible.

Trademarks are used to distinguish the goods and services of one business from that of another, so they protect the good-will and reputation of your business. Essential, right?

They also cover a wide range of features from brand names, slogans or strap lines, logos, sounds and even smells can be protected. Think "The future's bright… the future's…" I don't need to expand further. Think also the colour purple on Cadbury chocolate, or the sound of the roar of the lion when MGM's films start, Nike's swoosh, McDonald's golden arches. I think you get the gist, the power of a trademark for brand recognition is undoubtedly one of the strongest facets of any business. It sets you apart and the more distinctive the better. Coca-Cola wasn't a word before it became a trademark!

———

What do I need to do before I register a Trademark?

Due Diligence is a term we talk about a lot in company law. What it basically means is there are some really practical steps you can take before you make an application to register your trademark which will limit the risk of your application being rejected or of you receiving an objection. It will also provide you with peace of mind that the mark you have chosen isn't in use by someone else.

The first hurdle you need to get over when submitting an application for registration of a trademark is to make sure it is acceptable as a trademark to the Intellectual Property Office. When choosing your trademark as I mentioned above it needs to clearly distinguish your goods and services from the goods and services of others and it will be rejected if it isn't distinctive enough so be bold, think of a mark that is unlike any others, make up words if you can or combine obscure words to create a new meaning - the more unique the better.

Once you are sure of the mark you want to register have a look at Companies House website and do a name search to check if anybody else has a company registered with the same name as your mark. Then do a similar thing with domain search sites. If the names are available, buy them, buy the company name even if you do not at this stage wish to trade it as an active company, buy all the domains because it will prevent anyone else from being able to buy them and use them in the future but also because it's not unknown for others to monitor brands as they become more successful and buy up these assets for no reason other than to offer them for sale to you in the future where the costs will be significantly higher, if you reach that stage. I've had clients who've had to spend tens of thousands of pounds buying their own name back. It feels like a recurring theme here but not everyone operates with the same levels of integrity and there are people out there that would go and register your trademark simply to stop you having it, competitors for instance or those who would be willing to sell it to you.

Then, go to all the social media channels and register the handles for your proposed trademark so again no one else can use those.

By doing all of this work in the beginning, it will minimise the opportunity that people have to copy you and it ring fences the protection your brand has. Remember Ana at the start of the book? This made a huge difference when she had to handle infringements, she felt prepared and ready when issues came up.

Ok, so what's next?

Well, once you've done your due diligence and you're completely satisfied that your trademark is distinctive, available and that you will not be infringing on someone else's intellectual property, then you can start your online application. The application process is pretty straight-forward but you will need to identify the classes that you want your trademark to be registered into as you can't add more classifications at a later date - that would require a whole new trademark application and someone else could have registered the same mark into those other classifications in the meantime.

As part of the registration process, you must specify which classifications you would like your trademark to be registered under. Classifications are basically the different types of business products and services that relate to your business. There are 45 classes in total, one to thirty-five are product based, and thirty-five to forty-five are for service providers. You need to consider what your business does now, and the future products or services you might want to provide and then register into all of those classes. There's a fine line to be drawn here however, as applying into too many classes could leave you open to more objections, but too few won't give you the protection you need, so don't use a broad-brush approach, and try and register everywhere - keep it to what you need.

Another good tip is to download the paper application and do a draft application. That is a great way to familiarise yourself with the whole application and be sure you are not making any mistakes. Then simply copy your answers into the online form when you are satisfied you have completed all the information properly.

A standard application will cost £170. The application will include registration into one class, after that, you will be charged £50 for each additional class you register into. The potential cost of registering a Trademark is usually a block for people, especially when it comes to taking advice. Hopefully, this information will ease some of that fear as having a protected trademark is an extremely strong and valuable asset for your business.

———

Now let's take a look at Patents!

If you're a product-based business I am sure this is an aspect of protection you have toyed with. A patent is essentially a way to protect a new invention from other people copying.

The process of patenting is not to register the look of a product. It's protection and recording of the component parts that come together to create the product that you have invented, therefore, when you think of patents, think parts, not the end product itself. A great recent example of this is the iPhone and how it all works.

Registration of a Patent is a much more complex process. An important point to note if you are potentially considering patenting is that previous disclosure of your invention can hinder and sometimes prevent a successful application on the basis that it is not a new idea, therefore be sure to keep things under wraps until your application is submitted. Best practice would be to ask anyone who is working with you on the new invention to sign a Non-Disclosure Agreement, this also sometimes referred to as a Confidentiality Agreement, to prevent any early confidential leaks about the product to the wider market.

The registration process itself can also carry some risk because before the patent is finalised, the details of the patent become public knowledge when it is published by the Intellectual Property Office. Whilst this is further on in the timeline of the patent application, it has been known for entrepreneurs to monitor new patent applications coming through and with a few tweaks, get your product to the market before you. In fact, some big corporates have teams monitoring new patents coming through and will deliberately create a competing product with enough differences so as not to infringe on your patent but that are similar enough to dilute the exclusivity of your invention, so the increased exposure and risk of copycats is something to be mindful of.

The application process can take anywhere from two to five years to register, and the average cost is around £4000. However, depending on the amount of work involved and the product type this could increase. If you are in the product industry, and you are thinking about registering a patent do bear that in mind before you go all in.

Brand protection is an area of your business that you can mostly take control of yourself. Provided you arm yourself with all the knowledge and information you need and are sure that you understand the process you can do most of the work yourself without needing to use a lawyer, but I wouldn't say that is necessarily the case when it comes to patents. The investment and commitment to a patenting process is much more significant than for instance a trademark application and there is more opportunity for issues to arise or mistakes to be made so do take advice if this is a road you would like to go down. It is also useful to have a lawyer who already knows your product and application in the event that a potential infringer comes on the scene!

Imagine finding yourself in a situation where you are four years down the line, only to receive the news that the application has been denied on the grounds of its patentability, but its already out there in the public domain and open now for abuse and infringement by others. At this stage, you have lost both time and your financial investment, so having a good lawyer to do your due diligence and advise on the process upfront will be invaluable when it comes to getting the right outcome or even deciding if patenting is the right option for your invention. So, take advice, do your due diligence, and always keep a close eye on what's going on in the market around you.

Enforcing your Intellectual Property Rights;

I hope that by now you are starting to get a feel for the different options you have when it comes to protecting your brand and have somewhat of an understanding of the different types of Intellectual Property you hold in your business. The most frequent question I get asked is, without doubt, what do I do if someone is infringing on my rights?

Firstly, your position will always be stronger where your rights are registered so keep that in mind.

Also, make sure you keep records of all your registered rights. You may need to access those quickly if you see a would-be copycat.

One of the biggest hurdles to overcome before you feel ready to tackle an infringer is mindset. As with everything in business our mindset can hold us back so knowing you have the security of your registered rights will give you confidence, but it will only go so far. You have to be ready to take the steps necessary to protect and fight for your brand, and to do that will take courage. It will feel uncomfortable at first, difficult conversations and situations always are but they do get easier the more experience you gain. Making legal protection part of your everyday in business is essential. We have to go all in. You need to be willing to defend yourself and your business and often that won't happen until there is a very real risk that your brand is being diluted and that others actions are having a negative financial impact on you or causing damage to your reputation. Basically, when the shit is hitting the fan and you don't have any choice but to do something. The truth is however, if we let go of the fear of handling these situations properly right from the beginning, the likelihood of it ever really escalating to a point where your business is really at risk is much lower.

What actually happens if you don't take action from the beginning is that people get the impression that this stuff doesn't matter to you, and of course, that should never be the case. You and your brand deserve protection. All the time, effort, and money that you have put into creating and registering your Intellectual Property is wasted because if you do not follow through, people will see you as an easy target and continue to copy you.

But it is not just that is it? When you are running your own business, yes, some days will feel uncomfortable and almost too much to take on, but from what I have learnt through my own difficult times and from representing hundreds of clients over the years is that it is in those moments that we truly grow. It's where we really start to value our worth and what we have created and being willing to defend that will take you to a whole a new level of belief in yourself, so back yourself every single time.

Yes, it will feel out of your comfort zone and yes, it will feel scary, but that's ok. Take advice and take the steps you need to make sure you feel in control. I promise you; you will feel empowered and powerful. Don't let others piggyback off your success, they need to do their own work. It is all a journey, right?

Ok, so once you have dealt with the mindset side of things, and trust me it happens to the best of us, there are also some practical steps that you need to take:

The first is trying to prevent the infringement in the first place. We want people to know that we take our brand and protecting it seriously and registering your trademarks and design rights is the first step towards that, but what else can we do?

Let's start with Intellectual Property notices. What are they...? I hear you. Well, they are written notices that serve as a warning to others that copyright, trademarks, or design rights exists. This would also apply to patents. Those notices should be displayed on your website and all of your social media accounts to act as a deterrent to wannabe copycats.

The posting of a copyright notice itself is not a legal requirement. As we have seen copyright is an unregistered right that arises automatically if the requirements for its existence are met. However, a copyright notice will inform the public that the work is protected by copyright and it identifies the copyright owner, shows the year of first publication which as a result may assist you evidentially if your work is infringed and could limit the risk of the defence of innocent infringement being claimed.

These can also be included in your terms and conditions, on the bottom of your emails and in any workshops or materials you share with your clients or prospective clients. If you think about the information you share in marketing materials such as lead magnets, these are easily at risk of copying however including Intellectual property notices it may just make people think twice. I've included some of these in the free resources section on my website, so be sure to go and download those via the link in the back of this book.

Another practical step you could take is to monitor your registered rights. Registration is the first step, and I would suggest that at least every three months that either you or someone who works for you does a sweep of the internet to check if your protected marks are being used or if your copyright is being infringed. Do a Google search, check Facebook, Instagram, Twitter and anywhere else that your competitors could be promoting themselves. Look to see if anyone is using your words, slogans, or the names of your products and keep a record of those details, you never know when they may provide valuable evidence.

If you discover that your intellectual property has been stolen or is being used without your permission the first thing you should do is ask them to stop, this could be just an email or through a direct message being clear of what rights are being infringed.

This doesn't have to be heavy handed communication at this stage, the aim is to open up the line of communication and try to resolve the problem. I believe that we can have these conversations without there needing to be a huge fall out. Nine times out of ten, when you take this action and someone checks you out, they will stop using it because it is either a genuine mistake or they were just chancing their luck and in fact, love what you do. In the online world, we are constantly consuming and being "inspired" by others so the line can sometimes feel very blurred when working out what you have created and what you saw online a few days before! Evidence in these situations however will always be key.

Another key tip will be date stamping all of your copyrighted work so that you can evidence your length of use, should someone argue that they had the idea first.

———

But what happens when they don't stop?

When they don't stop you need to consider taking formal action. I know, I know... this is not the road you want to be going down and I agree we should try to avoid resorting to the courts as much as possible that's why, early protection and planning is so important when it comes to legals but sometimes it will be unavoidable.

The formal process is instigated by sending a cease-and-desist letter which can often have the desired effect of stopping the infringer without a dispute escalating. A carefully drafted cease and desist is a useful tool, especially if you are up against a business where the likelihood of recovering your legal costs should it go to court is low.

You also have the option of applying to court for an injunction, which is an urgent remedy to put a stop to the action or at least prevent it from getting worse until you are at a stage where you can claim damages or reach a settlement. While a court order will inevitably get you the right outcome if successful, this is a higher risk option than sending a cease and desist as the outcome is not guaranteed and the costs are likely to be much higher.

When materials are being published online, there is another option of directing your action at the internet service provider who will serve a copyright breach notice on the individual and in theory, should remove the content, the caveat to this being that it will always be dependent on individual circumstances.

While there are various options you can take to handle infringement. Sadly, sometimes a dispute will be unavoidable, and it is at this point that you need to carefully weigh up the benefits of pursuing a claim through the courts.

Cases such as these can run into tens of thousands of pounds in legal costs and take many months to get to trial, therefore this is not a decision to take lightly. You should always take legal advice on the details of your case as it is not a "one size fits all" approach. The approach you take will be dependent on the type of intellectual property being infringed and whether the right is registered at the Intellectual Property Office.

What a lawyer will be considering for you is the strategy needed to ensure the best possible chance of success for your claim. Litigating will always require a tactical approach, dependent on the particular facts of a case, and with intellectual property, the risks are high because the stakes are high - and the value of the claims follow that. Therefore, as we touched on before, making sure you have evidence is key, so be sure to keep date stamped screen shots of any infringing material you come across, as you lawyer will need it. If you are successful, the outcome will be damages or injunction and an award for costs. However, if you lose, your costs are unlikely to be recoverable.

Often there will be opportunities to reach a settlement at various stages of the process, and this is always an advisable option as it will cap your exposure to mounting legal costs but also avoid escalation of the dispute that can be tough on your emotional well-being. I have worked with many clients over the years who find the stress of the legal process difficult to cope with. It's not easy trying to keep going every day with the weight of litigation and potentially mounting legal costs over you and it can easily have a detrimental impact on you and your business. Always have an open mind and take on board the advice of your lawyer; if they propose a settlement to you, they will be doing it with all of the facts in mind and with experience of what the likely outcome to you claim will be. A court will also encourage an out of court settlement and a well drafted settlement agreement will also make it easier for you to obtain an injunction against the infringer if they breach your intellectual property again.

How to make your Intellectual Property work for you?

Having created and protected your intellectual property rights, you may at some point in the future be thinking of ways to expand your business and commercialising your brand may be a good option. What I mean by that is using your brand itself to generate more income and there are a few ways that can happen.

The first would be by licensing your brand and associated intellectual property to others to use. A licence would generate a profit-sharing mechanism where your licensee would pay you money for the use of your brand and the goodwill you have attached to it under specific terms that would be agreed in a licence document... yes, another contract! This is not an exclusive arrangement as of course; you want the freedom to offer licence to as many people as possible to grow your brand and generate more turnover. Franchising is also an option, but in a franchise model, it is usually the whole of a businesses operating procedures, plus the intellectual property that is shared, whereas with a licence model, it is usually just the brand.

———

What other forms of protection should I have in place for my brand?

Let's have a think about when you commission people to do work for you, for instance, if you have someone do design work on your brand or maybe a copywriter to help you with your messaging, but it could be anyone that you engage as a contractor for your business. It's worth noting here that this doesn't apply to employees provided you have the proper provisions in your employment contracts.

Before you start working with anyone of course, the terms and conditions under which they will be providing services are really important. In those terms, you need to be sure that the appropriate clauses are included transferring the intellectual property rights in the work they are doing for you, to you.

There is a common misconception that if you pay or commission someone to do work for you, that you will automatically acquire the intellectual property rights in that work. Sadly, that's just not the case. Without the proper protection of a contract, those rights will remain with the original owner of the work, being the person, you are paying to work for you.

The best position you will want to achieve at the end of the contract is that intellectual property rights are transferred to you absolutely, meaning you acquire full ownership. This will certainly be required if you are planning to trademark a new brand, for instance. Other rights that may be granted include licence rights, but you need to be very clear, and understand what rights are being granted to you because licenses are basically permission to use the work in certain circumstances.

It so easy to get caught up in the excitement of working with a new person that often things like this can get missed, and that can be hugely damaging to the value of your brand. High profile cases have come through the courts for this very reason and there is no guarantee that you will acquire title to the work if you bring a claim.

Another important factor for brand protection is having people that you share business information with sign non-disclosure agreements (NDA), also sometimes referred to as Confidentiality Agreements. The purpose of the NDA is to obtain clear contract terms confirming that your intellectual property and confidential information won't be shared with anyone outside of the contract.

There is a lot to think about when it comes to protecting your brand, but it is a highly valuable and integral part of your business and needs to be given conscious thought when setting out your brand strategy. A successful entrepreneur will gain a competitive edge with the proper protections in place. It makes for a long-term presence in the market and much greater brand recognition.

By arming yourself with an understanding of what intellectual property rights you own, protecting those rights where possible and utilising the benefit of those rights to build your business and brand, you won't go far wrong.

CHAPTER 4

PUT IT IN WRITING

LET'S TALK CONTRACTS!

R emember Eva? Let's just recap on her situation, she didn't have a proper contract in place with her client who brought a claim against her, so when the time came, she found it extremely difficult to prove what was agreed at the beginning of the relationship - the expectations were too vague and the services being offered weren't clear enough, so it was so much harder to satisfy a judge on her view of the dispute.

Your businesses potential for making money hinges on the relationships that you form, from those with your suppliers right through to your clients, and/or customers. Those contractual relationships whether they are in writing or made verbally are fundamental to its success so leaving yourself exposed by properly protecting yourself with clear terms could be catastrophic.

Every sale or purchase relationship you have in business will start with some form of agreement and unless you have the in house expertise to be able to do all the things you will be negotiating terms with many different people throughout your business journey. For instance when you are setting up your website you may need to find someone to help you design it, for that you will need a website design and development agreement, there will be a separate agreement for the hosting, what if you want to create an app for you may need to negotiate a mile app development agreement and then an end user licence agreement to sell it on to your customers or you might even want to work with someone to optimise your SEO - all of these agreements will have specific terms that relate to them so there really is no getting away from contracts, terms and conditions, agreements, whatever you call them as much as we would all like to.

As an online business owner with undoubtedly a website there is certain information that you must provide to the public in order to comply with UK law. On your homepage for example you should links out to a set of website terms and conditions that include, amongst other things, details of how people should interact with the site, regulation around unauthorised use of your content and unacceptable user behaviour such as hacking and viruses.

You are also required to have a link to your privacy policy and cookie policies to be compliant with data protection legislation The Privacy and Electronic communications Regulations 2003. Any website owner that collects personal data will be deemed under the General Data Protection Regulation and the Data Protection Act 2018 a "controller" of personal data and with that comes responsibility. You have an obligation to provide your data subjects (those people who's data you are collecting) with fair processing information which is usually done in a privacy policy or notice and includes information about what information you collect, who's data you are collecting, how and why it is held and if you are profiling that information. If your site is collecting personal data such as names, contact details and payment information about your online users then you will have to comply with data protection rules or you could find yourself subject to a fine so be sure to have your privacy policies and cookie policies in place and review them regularly to make sure they reflect how you operate in your business. I know the temptation is to put these things in place once, never to be looked at again but your business evolves just as you do so review them every few years and be sure to have robust security procedures in place if you intend to collect and use personal data.

Another point for you to consider with your website is if it links out to other sites, whilst this may not be of great concern to you, it is best practice for you to consider what will happen if the links out to other sites have undesirable material. What if your brands aren't aligned or even worse the content is misleading or inappropriate, in practice yes thats difficult to control but creating links without specific permissions in place covering the type of content you agree to share and kink could leave you exposed so consider if you need to give specific permissions or have standard website linking licence included in your terms.

Even just from the standpoint of setting up your online business you can see that there are a lot of things to consider that may feel overwhelming, just keep in mind that they all link back to the greater good of preserving and protecting your interests and while yes on times doing all of this stuff will just feel boring it will most definitely pay dividends in the long run.

———

Let's think for a second about content. Creating it, sharing it, acquiring it, it's a fundamental part of any online business and requires maybe a little bit more thought than perhaps you may at first realise. The creation of your content is covered by copyright that we discuss in detail in chapter 3 but what about when it's not created specifically by you? What happens then?

When you have employees the position is quite straight forward in that any content created by one of your employees during the course of their employment belongs to the employer, this can on times be questioned if content creation is not covered by their job description so be sure to include that but on the whole anything your employees create will be owner by you and this should also be covered in their employment contract.

What about however when you commission others to create content for you, those not employed by you? Maybe a web designer, copywriter, social media manager, designer who are not part of your business. You will need to remember here that unless there is a clear agreement in place by way of a written contract transferring ownership of that content to you then ownership remains under the laws of copyright with the person who created it so be sure to protect yourself here.

Another way for a business owner to acquire rights to content is to negotiate a licence of it. If you want to use other peoples content whether thats written, video, audio whatever it looks like you need to have their permission and this is usually documented by a licence which is effectively granting you a permission to use it for specific purposes. If you intend to stream live content the rules are the same, again you need permission so it will always be best practice and safer to have that permission in writing.

———

But let's go right back to the beginning and think about what a contract actually is and how they come about?

In short, it is an agreement between two parties. That's it. Whether it's on the back of a cigarette packet (I'm not sure that's a socially acceptable analogy these days but hey, I was dancing my way through the nineties, so I'll go with it), a verbal agreement or an email exchange. The actual existence of a formal written document isn't necessary and the courts will recognise a contract, even in the most obscure situations if two parties have shown a clear informed intention to reach an agreement, so it's so important for you to have control over the terms you want to be bound by, as otherwise default terms will be implied into your agreement.

When does a contract come into existence?

This is important because it determines when your customer becomes legally bound to buy from you, or vice versa, for you to provide services or goods and ordinary contractual principles apply to electronic communications so whether your trading online or offline the formation of a proper contract is subject to the same rules. What often happens however is that the parties fail to recognise the existence of a contract or when it became legally binding, incorrectly working on the assumption that it is ok to change their mind and simply walk away and sadly that is not always the case.

What if a conversation took place between two parties, let's say in January, for a programme or course starting in July? Under English law the general rule is that a contract is formed when the offer is accepted by the buyer and there is an intention to form a contract, additionally in e-commerce selling that there is sufficient certainty of the terms that have been agreed. Anything leading up to that point is just a nego-tiation between two parties and either can walk away.

The position when determining if a legally binding agree-ment has been formed therefore between you and another is to consider whether there has been an offer, acceptance of that offer, consideration, an intention to create a legal relationship and sufficient certainty of the terms that have been agreed. Without those elements the existence of a contract is unlikely.

Despite the huge growth in the e-commerce sector there is still not clear guidance under English law of how the rules of offer and acceptance should be interpreted when contracts are formed using internet based methods of communication. If you are unsure best practice would be to consider all of the circumstances and the context for the particular arrangement, for instance a zoom call is likely to be deemed as similar to face to face selling whereas email or text may be closer to the rules for written offer and acceptance are dealt with in writing.

In our scenario, when you have provided the details of what you are selling to a customer giving them enough information to make an informed decision (offer) and they communicate a positive acceptance of that decision to you (acceptance) and subsequently pay a deposit (consideration), it is safe to assume that their intention is to create a legal relationship with you and this is when the contract is formed and becomes legally binding.

Whether or not that contract is confirmed in writing is irrelevant and while it will always be preferable to confirm your terms in writing a contract will also come into existence when an agreement is made verbally. What can happen however is that the absence of a formal written contract leaves business owners unsure of their position and they therefore don't feel confident to confirm that the agreement has already become contractual - the best way to make sure the proper and intended terms are being agreed to and that your buyer understands that they have entered into a legally binding agreement with you at that point is to PUT IT IN WRITING.

I joked to a client recently that I was going to get t-shirts printed with "PUT IT IN WRITING" on as I say it so often, but it's actually the most important message I can give you so if you take anything away from this book, please let it be this point. (I'm sure I have said that in every chapter...) Your business is built on every agreement you enter into. I know it sounds dramatic and can feel like this doesn't apply to you, but remember Eva in the beginning of the book. The risks to you are unlimited if something goes wrong because you can't prove what was agreed between you and didn't have the proper protections in place to limit your liability which could spark the beginning of the end of your business, and I don't want that for you.

It's not just your clients that need a contract though... do you collaborate with other business owners? Do you buy from suppliers? Do you work with freelancers? Do you have employees? Do you work with affiliates? Do you collect people's data? Do you need investment? Every single one of those parts of your business need a contract of some form so don't get caught out.

Once you've established that you need a contract, it's time to decide what that contract will look like.

———

Let's take a more detailed look at our client or customer contracts.

This is where the other party becomes really relevant because what you're selling, and to whom, and from where, will determine the type of contract or terms and conditions (and all of these terms are interchangeable - you will hear me talking about contracts, terms, T&C'S, agreements, and they all mean exactly the same thing - they are all contracts) that you need.

When working out who you are selling to, the question to ask yourself is whether your customers buy your goods or services in connection with their trade, business, profession, or career. If they do, then you are selling to a business (B2B). And yes (I hear you) this applies even if they are individuals contracting in their personal name, remember the potential risks from personal liability we talked about earlier?

If they are buying your goods or services from you for their own personal use, then this is a consumer led transaction. (B2C)

But you might be wondering, why this is important? Under consumer law, consumers get better protection than businesses, generally because with business to business the perception is that the parties will be contracting on an equal footing. We have a greater duty of care to our consumers so for that reason, you will need to use different terms and conditions to ensure you are legally compliant. It's worth noting here that if you sell to both consumers and businesses then you will need to have two sets of terms and conditions or a really robust set that covers both.

Next, think about what it is you are selling - is it goods, services, or mixture of the two? Or it could be that you are selling digital content through downloads, in which case special rules apply and I will cover that a little later on.

———

Let's start with selling to Consumers ('B2C').

Businesses selling online must develop their sales process and online presence to comply with the rules around distance selling and e-commerce and particular information must be given to consumers at the right times to avoid extended cancellation periods and potentially other sanctions. Before we start I think it will be useful to confirm to you the bulk of the legislation that applies when you are selling to consumers, this is not an area of business to take lightly as the rules governing how we must deal with consumers is highly regulated. Im not here to scare you but equally its so important for you to understand the risks and regulations that apply.

So what is the core legislation that applies;

Not surprisingly to you I am sure, the Consumer Rights Act 2015 is a fundamental piece of legislation in this area and sets out the keys rights consumers have in respect of contracts for the sale and supply of goods, services and digital content.

It includes provisions specific to what you are selling with governing terms on the differences between how you should handle the sale of goods, services or digital content depending on what your business sells. Terms that will be implied into consumer contracts even when not expressly stated in your terms, a consumers remedies if you do not conform to the correct standards, rules on what would be considered an unfair term, delivery requirements, when the risk in a product will pass to your buyer, consumer guarantees and many other provisions that your terms and conditions should include.

Another key piece of legislation is the Consumer Contracts (Information Cancellation and Additional Charges) Regulations 2013. This deals with the information that you as a trader must provide to a consumer before they enter into a contract with you and the information that must be provided when the contract has been concluded. The cancellation rights that will apply to the contract throughout the cancellation period, what additional fees are allowed and the ongoing service obligations you have to your consumers (after sales).

You also need to be aware of the provisions of the Consumer Protection from Unfair Practices Regulations 2008. These regulations restrict unfair commercial practices by business owners that could have a detrimental impact on a consumer and cover issues such as misleading consumers either by giving them incorrect information or omitting to give them full and proper information. It also covers aggressive and other banned practices, which to get wrong could in more serious cases lead to criminal sanctions.

The Consumer Rights (Payment Surcharge) Regulations 2012 prohibit sellers from charging fees over and above the sale price advertised because of the payment methods chosen by the Buyer.

When advertising in your business you should also be aware of the Business Protection from Misleading Marketing Regulations 2008. These regulations are primarily concerned with business to business contracts however they also offer comparative guidance on permitted marketing practices to consumers.

Data protection legislation included General Data Protection Regulation ("GDPR"), Data Protection Act 2018 ("DPA") and the Privacy and Electronic Communications Regulations 2003 ("PECR") deal with consumers data protection and e-privacy generally. GDPR governs the general processing of personal data and so needs consideration as I am sure you are aware when collecting, handling, storing and processing data. The DPA has a number of detailed provisions in situations outside of the scope of GDPR and then PECR is particularly important to consider from a consumer protection perspective when you are advertising online using cookies or other similar technology and when you are direct marketing to consumers. It also regulates any form of unsolicited by electronic means such as email.

Now lets look at the E-commerce Regulations 2002. These regulations apply to most businesses that share information online about their products and services and or sell goods or services over the internet or via email. It requires you to provide certain and specific information to your customers and we will detail that a little further on in this chapter.

Where you are a business that deals with products the rules covered by the Consumer Protection Act 1987 set out your liability for when products are defective and provides for the making and enforcement of safety regulations particularly when it comes to the sales of cosmetics, clothing and toys etc and the General Product Safety Regulations 2005 set out a general product safety requirement that calls for you to only place products on the market if you can be sure of their safety. Other legislation that is specific to your product industry will also apply of course and in those case the industry specific regulation will override the more general provisions.

If you are a service based business you will also need to consider the impact of the Provision of Services Regulations 2009 that apply to any service provider, whether you are an individual or company, that provides a service that you charge for in the UK. It is also worth noting here that providing a service will also apply to the activity of retail trade therefore these regulations are likely to apply to you. You are required to supply various information (some automatically and other parts on request), must also deal with complaints as quickly as possible and make real (best) efforts to find a satisfactory solution to a customer complaint (there is a caveat here for purely malicious or vexations complaints) and you may not, in general, include discriminatory practices that may prevent those anyone from accessing your services. The Equality Act 2010 also deals with discrimination when contracting with those who have protected characteristics.

If you are trading as a Company as opposed to being a sole trader, as we dealt with earlier, you have additional disclosure requirements to take into consideration, referred to as 'trading disclosures'. Trading disclosures require you to display the company registered name, number and registered office on your website (as an online business) or at a trading address if you operate offline. Your registered name also needs to be disclosed on all correspondence or publications, order forms. There are also other requirements such as the obligation to provide details of share capital, directors details and registered office details to Companies House and any failure to comply with the trading disclosure requirements could lead to not just civil action being taken against you but also in more serous cases criminal liability could arise. While the regulation is strict in this area as with many others the likely outcome if you were found to not have put the correct trading disclosures in place is that you would be told to rectify, I am yet to hear of formal action being taken against a company simply because of a failure to put the right information in their trading disclosures but the risk is still there.

Another key piece of legislation that could have an impact on your business is the Consumer Credit Act 1974 and I am sure you have come across the Section 75 rules that apply when customers pay with a credit card. In this situation the credit card company becomes jointly and severally liable for a breach of contract or misrepresentation by you. In these circumstances consumers can make a claim against the credit card company as opposed to against you directly, which is of course very useful if or when a company becomes insolvent so a claim against them would be of no value.

The Misrepresentation Act 1967 is also relevant to you. A misrepresentation that we cover a little further on is a statement of fact made by one person to another that induces the other party to enter into a contract and it applies whether you are dealing with businesses or consumers.

As you can see there is a whole host of legislation (the above list not being exhaustive) thats applies when you are contracting with consumers that you must consider when implementing your terms and conditions. And, even more importantly why terms and conditions are absolutely necessary in your business.

———

Running an online business often means that there are also additional provisions that you will need to consider. Assuming, that all of your contract negotiations take place via the internet, phone, zoom, or online via a website, you are 99% of the time going to fall into the category of e-commerce and distance selling, but if you also trade in different ways, bear this in mind as you may need to make further tweaks to your terms, and I suggest you get advice on your particular circumstances from a lawyer.

You will be aware as a consumer yourself that today's world pretty much gives us the option to buy anything online, change your mind and send it back, but what you might not be aware of is the impact that can have on your business as an online seller.

A distance selling contract, in its most basic form, is a contract made between a buyer and a seller away from the business premises of a supplier, that includes internet sales, and particular rules governing consumer sales will then apply. A consumer, as we touched on before, is someone who is operating outside of a business, and when a business enters into a contract for supply with a consumer, they must provide the customer with certain information, including clear, unambiguous information about the right to cancel and return the goods, the terms of which will depend on whether you're supplying goods, services, or digital content, such as apps and digital downloads.

Consumer terms and conditions, when drafted for you, will on the whole follow a format to ensure you are meeting all of your obligations under the Consumer Rights Act 2015 and any associated regulations, but it will depend on what it is your business sells. If you are running a consumer led business generally consumers have 14 days in which to change their mind and receive a refund for the cost of the goods and the cost of delivery to the customer. There are some caveats to this, for instance, if you determine that the goods have been handled more than is necessary - and what would usually be deemed necessary would be similar to how you would expect goods to be after someone has tried them on in a shop - then as the supplier, you may be able to make a reduction in the refund to reflect the reduced value of the goods.

Also, if the customer has consented or insisted on services being provided during the cancellation period and then wants to rely on the 14-day cooling off period the supplier is entitled to payment for the services that have been already delivered up to the date of cancellation provided that a waiver is included in your terms and conditions.

So, if your business sells to individual consumers that you don't meet in person, either because you have an online business or your business simply doesn't trade out of traditional business premises, it's really important that you're aware of the additional consumer rights that apply to these kinds of 'distance sales' to avoid any costly mistakes.

So, what do you need to have in your terms?

Under the Consumer Contracts (Information and Cancellation and Additional Charges) Regulations you are required you to give the following minimum information to your customers before you enter into a sale, this includes: your business name, contact details and address, a description of your goods or services, the price - including all taxes, how your customer can pay, what your delivery arrangements are, the delivery costs and how long goods (if your selling goods will take to arrive), the minimum length of their contract and billing period (if it's not a one-off sale), conditions for ending the contract, guarantees that apply to the products or service, how and when they can cancel and, if relevant, when they lose the right to cancel, if they will be subject to further costs if they cancel, a cancellations form and clear unequivocal instructions of how they cancel.

All of this information must be easy to understand and in a format the customer can save for future reference. Therefore, having a set of terms and conditions when dealing with consumers is not just a nice-to-have, they are an absolute essential if you want to avoid penalties, fines and potentially, worst case scenario, being closed down by trading standards.

Another pre-requisite is that delivery is achieved within 30 days unless a different time frame has been agreed with your customer.

But let's talk a little bit more about the right to cancel. You have a legal obligation as an online business owner to tell customers that they can cancel their order for a period of 14 days from the date of sale or, if it's goods, they can cancel their order for up to14 days after their order is delivered and they don't have to have to give you a reason for doing this! Now, I know that it feels a little unfair and is probably a nerve-wracking thought when you have worked so hard to find and nurture your customers to get the sale that they can then just change their minds, but you have also probably come across some pretty full on and, in some cases, down-right dodgy sales tactics, where customers feel pushed into a sale, so this time serves as a cooling off period to limit the risks to buyers.

Don't be fooled into thinking you can keep quiet about this right and hope it won't apply. If you don't tell your customers in your terms and conditions that they have a right to cancel, you're leaving your business exposed to even more risk because, as we have said above, they must be given this information upfront and if you don't tell them, then that right to cancel is extended to any time in the next 12 months! So don't get caught out with this one and make sure you have this in your terms. If you realise you have made a mistake and not given this information, you can tell them at any time, and they will then have 14 days from being told that they have the right to cancel. There are however some situations where the cooling off period doesn't apply, including when:

- Goods that are prone to deteriorate or are perishable
- Goods with fluctuating prices
- Newspapers and magazines
- Betting and gambling services
- Goods that are made to a customer's order, for example, tailored clothing
- Accommodation, transport, food and drink and leisure services that are provided for a specific event, or on a particular date, or within a specified period
- Day-to-day food and drink, delivered house to house
- Package travel and timeshares
- Software, CDs, and similar items that have been unsealed
- Digital downloads once the download process has started

So, if your client or customer asks you for a refund and it's within the cooling off period, and none of the above exemptions apply, then you have to refund them within 14 days of the request to comply with the regulations, so do make a note of that.

———

What's different about digital content?

It's, of course, in a seller's favour to have the right to the 14 days cooling off period waived when selling digital content because otherwise content could be used, downloaded, and consumed within that period very easily and it's difficult to prove otherwise. Additional rules therefore apply, when a business sells digital services that are downloaded or streamed live online that need to be included in your terms and conditions to gain the benefit of, which is why it is so important to make sure you have the correct terms applicable to what you are selling. If you are a business owner that supplies downloads or live streaming then you must be sure to include terms confirming that the customer will lose their right to the 14-day cooling off period and that they are agreeing to receive an instant download, because if you don't provide this information then the 14-day rule will still apply. Are you still with me?

This is one of the more complicated parts of running an online business as there are so many ways that you can get caught out so don't beat yourself up if you haven't got this quite right until now. You don't know what you don't know, right. Its about arming yourself with the knowledge so that going forward you can be sure that you are protected and have the right terms in place.

What then happens outside of the 14-day cooling off period?

The Consumer Rights Act 2015 sets out the rules you need to follow and those rules are different depending on what it is you sell. Remember we are still dealing with consumers here so this is not relevant for business to business contracts.

If you are selling goods, the legislation has pretty much followed the previous standards applied under the Sale of Goods Act 1979, in that good must be of satisfactory quality, fit for purpose and be as described when marketing or advertising. Goods must also match the image or model that was shown to the consumer to try and get the sale, unless the seller has brought the differences to the consumer's attention before the contract is made. Where goods are installed for people, they will not meet the required standards if they have been installed incorrectly and if goods include digital content, such as downloads, the goods will not comply with the standards if the digital content doesn't match what's in the contract.

The remedies that buyers are entitled to in these circumstances, for instance where goods do not conform with the contract, and the standards are not met, are then tiered. Assuming that the 14-day cooling off period has passed, the consumer can ask the trader to repair or replace the goods.

If repair or replacement are impossible or the repair is inadequate, the consumer can then ask for the price to be reduced or they have a final right to reject the goods.

The final right to reject allows for the refund to the consumer to be reduced by a deduction for use, to take account of the use that the consumer has had of the goods since they were delivered to them. There is an assumption however that if the issue has arisen in the first 6 months of receipt of the goods, then it is likely to have been there at the time of purchase.

When selling services, the rules are slightly different.

The Consumer Rights Act 2015 provides that services must be performed with reasonable care and skill and in accordance with the information provided prior to the contract becoming legally binding. Where no price is specified, services must be provided for a reasonable price and where no date or time period is specified, services must be performed within a reasonable time.

Now, you are probably thinking, what is reasonable skill? You are not alone. It's the answer that lawyers have been searching for since the beginning of time. It will be interpreted differently by different people but that was exactly the intention of the legislation to allow flexibility between different sectors and industries as, of course, what is reasonable for a qualified professional, for example, won't be the same as for an administrative assistant. If your client complains that they feel they have not received the level of service they expected, then you, as the business owner, need to be as objective as possible and take into consideration what would be a reasonable expectation of service level across your industry. Usually, you will know if your service wasn't up to scratch and can come to this conclusion quite quickly. If you determine that the client or customer has reasonable grounds for being unhappy with the service, what you should then do is offer to repeat the service or offer a partial refund. There is no hard and fast rule here, the guidance suggests that the refund would generally be the difference in the value of the service sold compared to the level of service received, but it is entirely dependent on the facts of each individual case. If however you determine that you have complied with the level of service you promised then you have the option to decline and confirm that the complaint is not upheld.

This area of law is vast, in fact it could be the subject matter of its own book, not just a chapter therefore if you are ever in doubt don't be afraid to take advice and check what will be relevant to your individual circumstances.

———

So, what if I operate purely business to business ('B2B')?

I mentioned above that a consumer is a person who is buying something for their individual or personal use but what is a business user? A business to business contract is when you are selling to a person or a company that is buying from you in the course of their trade, business profession or career, this is an important distinction to make when it comes to your terms and conditions. When you sell business to business the

Consumer Rights Act 2015 doesn't apply, and it is the standards set by the Sale of Goods Act 1979 and Supply of Goods and Services Act 1982 that therefore become relevant.

When you are selling online or via email, additional regulations, will also apply. The Electronic Commerce Regulations for instance govern situations where you are advertising and distance selling online. Those rules state that your business must date and make available to your buyers: your full business name, address and contact details, your VAT details where relevant, details of whether you are authorised by any profession or trade and any schemes that you belong to, but most importantly, your prices, applicable tax, and delivery costs of what it is you're selling therefore a good set of terms will always be required.

In addition to that, your business must make it clear in its terms any promotions, competitions or any conditions of purchase that apply to the sale.

Having proper terms will ensure that you cover off the essential information that you are required to give by law when running an online business, but it also manages the expectations of the parties and allows you to properly explore the whole relationship at the beginning of the customer journey rather than having to unpick what was intended if you find yourself dealing with a dispute later on.

Business to business contracts in comparison to business to consumer contracts vary quite substantially the reason being that the parties are deemed in the eyes of the law to be more sophisticated, in a stronger negotiating position and generally able to agree fair and reasonable terms. With consumers the selling business will always have a greater duty of care to ensure that their customers are not being placed at a disadvantage.

————

But what are the main differences you need to consider when selling business to business?

The rules regulating business to business sales are less restrictive and centre largely around fairness and acting reasonably. The Unfair Contract Terms Act 1977 places certain restrictions on businesses and prevents business sellers in particular being able to avoid liability for negligence or certain breaches of contract.

A supplier for instance in any circumstances (business or consumer) cannot include terms in their contracts that avoid liability for;

- Injury or death
- Negligence leading to unreasonable loss or damage
- Poor quality or faulty goods.

Within a business contract a term will be deemed to be unfair in certain situations such as;

- Where a term is not deemed to be made in "good faith". What is meant by that is that the law wants business owners to include terms in their contracts that meet certain standards of fairness and transparency.
- Where there is a significant imbalance of power, and a contract is too heavily weighted in favour of one party over another.

While the courts do not like to intervene in business to business contracts as the contracting parties are generally free to contract on whatever terms they choose, they will step in if they believe there is an element of unfairness so be sure to keep balance and fairness in mind when drafting your terms. That's not to say you can't keep commerciality at the heart of your contracts, you are in business to make a profit so do make sure you protect your time and efforts with a properly drafted set of terms.

By having specific terms set out in a proper business to business contract you can avoid the need to rely on rights implied by the courts or in law, what you agree with your customer will essentially become the binding terms provided they are not challenged. It is where there is no contract, and a dispute arises that the law will be required to step in and imply terms they feel would have been intended by the parties or in the absence of evidence to suggest what was intended, what would be reasonable in the circumstances and this may not always meet your expectations.

Certain terms are also implied by statute in particular under the Sale of Goods Act 1979 there will be implied into every contract unless those provisions have been overturned through specific negotiations between the parties, a term that the seller has the right to sell the goods, that the goods will correspond with their description, that they are of satisfactory quality and reasonably priced fit for purpose. There are many factors that would be automatically implied into your agreements unless you take action and specifically include the provisions that you wish to trade on.

A frequent mistake is when business owners selling to other business owners believe that the 14-day cooling off period applies. There is no automatic right to a refund in a business-to-business contracts therefore unless you as a business owner specifically decides to grant your clients a contractual right to a refund the rules do not apply. Generally, from the minute you sign a business contract you are bound to its terms so be sure before you enter into any contract that you are absolutely willing to commit to the deal.

———

But, when can you end a business contract?

Terminating a business-to-business contract and expecting a refund is a situation I also see happening a lot. There is a common misconception that if you are not happy with the goods or services that you have been provided or simply change your mind due to a change in circumstances, that you can simply request a refund or stop paying and sadly that's just not the case.

There are very limited situations where a party can terminate a commercial contract for instance where there is a clear termination clause allowing termination on notice. This can be either party or just one.

In addition, you may have a clause in a contract that also states that you can terminate for a serious or material breach. What constitutes a serious or material breach would usually be defined in the contract terms and again would be in limited circumstances. A clear definition of what the parties view as serious enough to warrant termination is preferable and makes the situation much more clear cut to know when these rights will arise - so for instance nonpayment by your customer if you are the supplier or services not being provided if you are a purchaser is likely to constitute a material breach but again it will always depend on the facts of the particular case - a trivial matter is unlikely to be serious enough but what's trivial to one can feel serious to another so you can see why this area of law can be misconstrued and why disputes are not uncommon. What that doesn't guarantee you is a full refund, yes you may be able to bring your agreement to an end but in the absence of agreement between you and the supplier or purchaser that money should be refunded then you may still need to go to court to get your money back.

Are you still with me.. we've got this!

If a supplier or a purchaser commits what is referred to as a repudiatory breach of the contract, being a breach that goes against the very heart of the contract. This usually relates to a breach of a strict condition in the correct or refusal to perform obligations under a contract or even where a contract has become impossible to commit to then the other party may be able to bring the contract to an end, but this will depend on the particular circumstances of each case, and you are likely to have to go to court to obtain a refund and prove the breach, if you cannot reach agreement with the other party.

Where the concept of 'Force Majeure" applies it will exempt the parties from liability and gives them the right to terminate the agreement if events beyond their reasonable control, which will usually be defined in the contract, occur.

Frustration may also be an option in very limited circumstances where a party is simply unable to perform on their side of the contract.

All of these remedies however will be a question of fact of the individual cases and will usually require the courts intervention if the parties cannot agree to bring the contract to an end.

In short what I am saying is do not simply assume that because you are unhappy and request a refund that a supplier is bound to repay you. This of course works both ways, do not assume that simply because an unhappy client requests a refund that you have to concede. The particular facts and what's included in your contract will always be relevant.

A significant issue arises when a party believes that the original contract was misrepresented to them, or mis-sold and in the online space this is easily done. We see all the hype of the potential results you can achieve from working with the right coach or mentor or doing the right work on yourself and in those situations you need to be very clear on the contractual terms you are signing up to. Often, we will expect to see disclaimers or exclusion clauses in the terms and conditions dismissing reliance on the claims made because of course those outcomes very rarely can be guaranteed so do your due diligence and make sure you are aware of the contractual terms you are being offered not the elaborate claims on a sales page.

In a misrepresentation claim it is worth noting that it is the responsibility of the purchaser to prove that the supplier has mis-sold or misrepresented the sale which can be a difficult task especially if you are purchasing off the back of a sales call. This is another reason why everything should be documented in writing as it may become evidence should something go wrong. In a successful misrepresentation claim a purchaser will be able to bring an agreement to an end and recover their losses but again this will need to be dealt with through the courts which can be costly and as always will come down to the facts of the individual case.

In practical terms the best way to deal with a potential refund situation with your client or customer is to build into your contract a mechanism for handling dissatisfaction. By making it clear in your contract how you will handle the situation you retain control and avoid the matter escalating to a full legal dispute. A good starting point is to ask for the issue to be put in writing to you and to allow you a reasonable period to review what's happened and provide a response - we cover this more comprehensively in Chapter 6. You are then able to take a view on the matter and decide if the purchaser is acting reasonably with their request for a refund. If you cannot reach an agreement the matter will inevitably end up in the hands of the court who will look firstly at the terms you agreed, then beyond that to whether or not those terms were in fact fair and reasonable in the circumstances and then if the contract has been performed as it should have been. All of that can become very expensive not to mention the stress and time it can take you away from building your business so always be willing to take a look at the bigger picture. Taking a reasonable approach in these situations is always advisable. If you feel your customer or client has merit in their claim as we said before try to put emotion aside and consider a discount, repeat of the service, exchange of the goods or eventually a refund. If, however on the other hand you are sure that you have done everything you set out to do in the contract and have acted reasonably in the circumstances do not feel pushed into providing a refund because you aren't sure of your legal position. If you are ever in doubt, take advice.

What other terms should I include in my B2B contracts?

Other terms you should include in your business contracts to ensure they give you the protection you need include a proper definition of the services or goods being sold, quantities and timelines for delivery. Set out the full duration of the agreement, think about whether it will be for a fixed period of time for a one-off project or will run on a rolling basis until terminated by either party, what notice periods would then be needed to activate that termination? Include clear payment terms, how much is to be paid and when payment is needed. Is VAT applicable? Will there be any additional costs to pay on top of the agreed fee, for instance to third parties? What happens if payment is late, charging interest on late payments is normal in these circumstances You will also want to include a provision that legal ownership (referred to in law as legal title) of the goods doesn't pass to the buyer until full payment has been received.

Include clear confidentiality terms making sure that both parties are aware of their obligations in relation to the information thats being shared. Have a clause that ensures both parties will comply with relevant data protection legislation. Think through and set out what will happen with the intellectual property in the product or service - how can it be used by the other party, will you retain all intellectual property rights or will they have a licence to use it or it may be that you will need to transfer title to the intellectual property to them completely - this could be relevant if you are being commissioned to do design work for someone. It all comes down to what you agree.

Clauses such as disclaimers that seek to limit or exclude the risk of legal action being pursued against you should also be included, and other terms such as limitation of liability clauses with appropriate carves outs relating to what cannot be excluded by law and caps of the potential limits of liability, dispute resolution provisions, is there a complaints procedure, do you need a non solicitation provision? The parties notice requirements and confirmation of which law will apply to the contract should also be included to ensure total clarity on what is being agreed and expected of the parties in the event of a dispute.

––––––––

What does the law say when it comes to disclaimers?

As we touched on previously the regulation of this area of law all centres around fairness, with consumers having additional protection against terms which would be perceived as unfair even when common law or statute could permit their use.

The Unfair Contract Terms Act 1977 (UCTA) aims to reduce unfair terms in contracts and Section 2 of the Act states that you can't limit or exclude liability for death or

personal injury caused by your negligence, in any circumstances, as we have covered above.

You would have undoubtedly seen contract terms that state
something along the lines of 'nothing in these terms excludes
any liability that cannot be excluded by law'.. or similar.

It is also unlawful to mislead consumers about their legal
rights under the Consumer Protection from Unfair Trading
Regulations 2008, which repealed the earlier Consumer
Transactions (Restrictions on Statements) Order 1976. This
statutory instrument made it an offence to use certain kinds
of unfair contract terms or notice.

In addition to that, contracts with consumers are governed
by the Unfair Terms in Consumer Contracts Regulations
1999 (UTCCR) and schedule 2 of the Regulations state that
the following would be unfair:

"excluding or limiting the legal liability of a seller or
supplier in the event of the death of a consumer or
personal injury to the latter resulting from an act or
omission of that seller or supplier"

A contract term can never legally have the effect of
excluding liability for death or injury caused by negligence in
the course of business, and such terms should not appear in
any contracts. As well as being unfair, they are also

misleading to the public and could leave you open to risk of prosecution for unfair commercial practice so again go cautiously in this area and check in on your terms.

More general disclaimers, for example those stating that a customer's use of equipment or premises is 'entirely at their own risk' even if they are not intended for that purpose are likely to be perceived as also seeking to cover liability for death or personal injury. It could be that you simply intend to stop consumers trying to sue for loss of or damage to their property where they have acted carelessly but the fact that the intention behind a term is more limited than its potential effects does not make it automatically fair.

Where a contract involves an inherently risky activity the use of warnings against hazards which provide clear guidelines and information, and make it very clear that the consumer needs to take sensible precautions may go some way in reducing the level of liability.

Arguably telling people they do something at their own risk is a limitation of liability in some case, and the OFT makes this point in its guidance on unfair terms. But you have to ensure that your terms are drafted correctly to achieve this benefit for instance in the case of an wellbeing event where you are seeking to limit liability for how people may feel after the event something along the following lines would be sensible;

"By attending this event, I agree that I will only take part if I am well and in good health. I understand that the organisers will take reasonable steps to promote my safety and that I must comply with all instructions given by the organisers and anyone else providing guidance at the event."

Disclaimers may be acceptable if they are subject to a provision stating that liability for loss or harm is not excluded or restricted where the supplier is at fault, or is disclaimed only where someone else, or a factor outside anyone's control, is to blame. However, a disclaimer covering problems caused by a trader's suppliers or subcontractors is sometimes regarded in the same way as one covering loss or damage caused directly by the trader's own fault because the courts will sometimes take the view that a consumer has no choice as to they enter into a contract with and therefore has no contractual rights enforceable against the third party supplier.

So as you can probably see the use of disclaimers is never going to be black and white, there is a great bug grey area, other than you can be sure that it will never be lawful to seek or attempt to evade responsibility for causing death or personal injury as a result of your negligence.

The best way to look at it, while also trying to protect you and your business to the best lengths possible is to never try to deprive your customers of compensation in any circumstances in which they would normally be entitled to it by law and if you are ever unsure of your position take advice.

———

Having standard terms and conditions or contracts in business-to-business relationships are a great way to ensure that all of your business dealings are on the same terms and the more specific you can make them, the better. They should fit the needs of your business and how you operate day to day, don't fear making your terms bespoke to you or taking advice. Having a clear understanding of what's in your terms and using those to manage your business dealings will give you a new level of confidence as a business owner and will make those difficult conversations much less scary.

Now, let's take a look at effective incorporation when trading online. I am sure you're wondering what on earth does that mean, right? This stuff is complicated enough (I promise you it get's easier so hang in there) but, for a set of terms and conditions to apply in any business relationship be that with another business or a consumer you have to ensure that they have been specifically agreed to by the other party or that the other party knew, at least of the existence of them. You need to make sure that you have given sufficient notice of your terms to the other party if you wish them to form part of the contract and, this will be a question of fact in each case.

To achieve effective incorporation it will always be best practice to have a wet signature on a document to ensure the other party irrevocably agrees to the terms that you are putting forward. There can be no question then of their intention to be bound by your terms, making life much easier should you find yourself in dispute.

Some laws of England and Wales still require that documents must be 'signed" for the contract to be valid and the courts have on times questioned whether an electronic document is in fact "in writing". In summary what they would be looking at to determine if an e-signature was valid is whether you can be sure that the correct person with the right authority has signed the contract with the intent for it to become legally binding so when using electronic signatures be sure to use a professional platform and where the document is included in the link and always be sure the person who you are sending the contract to have authority to sign.

In the context of e-commerce the issue of incorporation can get a little more technical because of course you are not dealing in person and often terms and conditions are set out on a webpage for your business. You may also have come across the terms 'click wrap' and 'browse wrap' terms.

A 'click wrap' agreement is where we see that buyers have to actively click an 'I agree' or similar button (or tick a box) to confirm their consent to a contract governing the supply of the relevant goods, services or content.

The 'Browse wrap' (or 'click free') approach is perceived legally as more unsafe. It attempts to impose terms simply by virtue of the fact that their use of your site deems acceptance of certain terms available. It is generally doubtful whether such terms would meet the requirements for an enforceable contract under English law so do try to steer away from those, where possible. Use of browse wrap terms in connection with an ordering process is not recommended.

What we need to be absolutely sure of when trading online or entering into any contract is that the terms we are wishing to do business on become part of our contract and you want to be sure that your contract parties has specifically agreed to them.

Your terms and conditions should ideally be visible on your website at all times but it is also essential that they become an integral part of the buying process. The best and safest practice will always be to ask the buying party to scroll through your online terms and to positively click on the 'I accept' button, before they are allowed to finalise the order.

Through using this framework you can be certain that;

- the parties agree the terms apply to the contract,
- the website address where the applicable terms can be found is referenced, and
- that your client or customer has access to download the documents for future reference

Leaving you less open to the risk of a dispute or non compliance with your legal requirements.

———

And a final note;

As an e-commerce trader you can use the checklist below to see the kind of documentation you need to implement in your business to limit your exposure to risk and keep you compliant;

- Website terms and conditions
- Acceptable Use policy - this is particularly relevant where you may have users contributing material or comments on your website.
- Terms and conditions of sale or supply relevant to what you sell.
- Privacy Notice
- Cookie Notice
- Copyright Notice
- About you/us page with contact details of who you are, where and how you can be contacted.

CHAPTER 5

WHAT TO DO IF SOMEONE TRIES TO DAMAGE YOUR REPUTATION?

(AND WHAT NOT TO DO...)

S top the press she's about to say it again... I know, I know but I will keep on saying it and I really do want you to remind yourself of this chapter because in the heat of what can be a potential defamation against you all logic will leave your thinking and emotion will most certainly take over. Defamation is probably the most emotive legal topic that you will encounter when running your online, or in fact any, business.

The truth is, yes there will be situations that test you to the nth degree, we're not built for criticism and having someone talk about you or your business in any way other than positively is distressing for even the most hardened entrepreneurs. When I speak to clients who believe they have been victim of defamation or are in fear of an imminent attack to their reputation, remaining calm is the last thing they want to do. They want to act, they want to retaliate and they want to do it now, and who can blame them, but it is not always that straight forward. When it comes to the legal position in these cases, there are a few things you need to consider before you make the decision to take legal action.

Defamation itself doesn't have a statutory definition but there are some key ingredients that need to be present in any case for a possible defamation to arise. So lets explore what a defamation is; In its most simplistic form it is the publication to others of a statement about you where the imputation from those words is capable of causing serious harm to your reputation and, that those words cannot be proven to be true or excusable by any valid defence.

A defamation can come in the form of either a libel or, less commonly, a slander. Libel being the permanent publication of a written statement about you, for instance in a newspaper, book or magazine and will also cover some less permanent situations, such as when people make comments online about you, for instance in a Facebook or twitter post. Slander is usually spoken statements and, on occasion, could also be a gesture.

Let's look at what publication means in a bit more detail; its essential in these cases that the statement about you has been actually communicated to a third party. Written publication requiring that the words must have been read and understood by the third party or parties and oral publication requires that the words must be apprehended and understood by a third party or parties.

There is a 1 year limitation period that applies in a case of defamation that can only be avoided in very certain limited circumstances when agreed by the courts so be sure to act within the 1 year period from the actual defamation or as it is referred to by the courts as the cause of action. Don't sit on these things and think you can come back to it later, gather your evidence and take early advice.

As we have all witnessed in recent years, the online cancel culture is on the rise with commenting and effectively shunning influencers who have done or said something which, in the opinion of those commenting, warrants the ending of their online presence, but it does leave people exposed to potential action when the comments and actions are so obvious and intentional. Defamation law is mainly concerned with the meaning of words rather than the words themselves so when a persons online post or content is perverted or skewed to infer other meanings often associated with racism sexism hate or discrimination legitimate opinions can often become illegal because of the negative meanings they are seeking to place on the original posters words and this leaves commenters open to potential defamation claims as the victim of the cancel culture might be able to legal action against the originator of the statement and anyone who repeats it.

———

So what is Defamation?

The defamation occurs when something that is written or said about you, which is untrue and has potential to cause a person to lower their opinion of you, makes disparaging comments about your business, exposes you to ridicule, contempt or hate from others or even causes you to be avoided by others. To qualify as a defamation, a statement must also cause you serious harm. This is objective and will depend on the specific circumstances of each individual case. When it's in relation to a business, serious harm is directly linked to the likelihood of serious financial loss. That means that the statement must have the potential to cause you a direct financial impact, in that it could cause you to lose clients, contracts or future work. It's not enough that a statement has hurt your feelings or that your pride is dented. I get it and I hear you when you want to retaliate in these situations, but I urge you to think carefully before stomping in.

Whether serious harm has been caused or is likely to be caused will depend on the specific circumstances of the situation and will be determined by the actual impact that the defamatory statement has had on you and your business. If you pursue a case through the courts - and hopefully you will never need to do this - the courts will look at certain factors to determine the strength of your case. These factors include things like how serious the statements made against you were, how many people were exposed to the comments - so if a comment is made to a small group of people in a private community, it is unlikely to have the same impact as a comment made in a public forum by someone who has thousands of followers - they will also consider the individual circumstances of each case and it's potential, relatively, to cause you serious harm. In extreme circumstances, serious reputational harm and/or financial loss will be so obvious that the evidence required will be minimal.

A cease-and-desist letter is the normal course of action sought when this happens, and the aim of that letter is to remove the content that you believe to be defamatory; to cease the publication of a statement and prevent/desist the author of that statement from defaming you further.

A professional and well written cease and desist letter is likely to significantly reduce the likelihood of having to go to court because the recipient will immediately be put on notice that you do not tolerate defamatory behaviour. At that point, they are forced to consider their position and the potential risk of litigation being started against them which, in cases such as these, can run onto tens of thousands of pounds. The letter is the first step in formal court proceedings so it's unlikely that a savvy recipient (or respondent, which is the legal term for a defending party to a claim) will ignore your correspondence so for that reason, a cease and desist in a powerful tool in the armoury of an Entrepreneur subject to a potential defamation. If, however, a person refuses, on receipt of a cease and desist, to remove the defamatory statement or publication then you will be able to show the courts that you sought to rectify the situation before issuing a claim. This is really important when it comes to the question of who is paying the costs of a case. Judges do not take kindly to claimants (i.e., the person issuing the claim) who use the court system as metaphorical hammer to batter someone over the head. The court will always want the parties in any case to have tried to reach a resolution before looking to the court for a decision, so be very careful when deciding at what point you want to engage the courts and always take professional legal advice on your case beforehand to avoid wasted time and costs.

So, we have looked at when you have got a case and when you should be thinking about taking action but when should you not?

Under the Defamation Act there are four main defences to a claim for defamation and having a defence will stop any action that you take against a respondent in its tracks. With that in mind you should carefully consider these defences before sending a cease and desist, and even more so before committing to the legal expense of issuing a claim.

The defences are Truth, Honest Opinion, Publication on a matter of public interest, and Privilege. So, let's break these down.

Truth is a complete defence to a claim for defamation if the respondent can show that what they have published is substantially true. Now, it is not always that straight-forward.

As you would imagine, the person who wrote the defamatory statement has to prove, on a balance of probabilities, to a court, that they were true, rather than for the claimant to prove that they were untrue. In other countries, the onus is mores on the claimant to prove that they were untrue but the legal system here in the UK gives claimants an advantage.

Honest Opinion is also a defence and I am sure you have come across many situations where you have heard the words 'well I'm entitled to my opinion" and on the whole, that is true. To rely on this defence however, the publisher of the defamatory statement must be able to show that what they published was in fact, a statement of opinion, meaning that they need to be able to prove that an honest person could have held the same opinion based on the facts relevant to the particular circumstances and the only way to over-come this is to show, with no uncertainty, that the defendant did not hold that opinion. I'm sure you can appreciate the complexities of this situation, as proving what opinion someone truthfully held of you is a minefield.

Publication as a defence deals with situations where the person making the potentially defamatory statement believes that it was a matter of public interest that they shared their views. To rely on this defence however, they must be able to prove that it was a matter of public interest and not just that it is their opinion that it was in the public's interest, which is a different situation all together. This defence will generally be looking at whether or not by publishing the statement, it benefitted the public at large and not just a small section of it, so will be entirely dependent on the circumstances of the individual case. I am sure if we think about some of the behaviours of our current government, you can imagine when a defence such as publication will apply, but the test will be how many benefit.

And finally, Privilege. This is where public policy, for instance, speaking in parliament, protects statements made. The aim being that speakers are encouraged to speak openly and freely in those circumstances, and this will also apply in a court setting when giving evidence.

So those are the defences that may be available to you if you are on the wrong side of a claim for defamation but do also bear them in mind before you issue a claim against someone who has made a potentially defamatory statement against you. Going into a claim is not something to take lightly; the costs are high and the emotion of it all runs even higher. Cases can last for a number of years and the stress of that situation can easily take its toll. Always go through a risk benefit exercise with yourself and be sure that it is a fight that you want to enter into - from either side. Would your time and finances be put to better use in building your business is something I always ask clients to consider, it's a question only you can answer but, in my opinion, pride will never be justification enough.

Usually, if your defamation is successful either at court or in a settlement out of court, you will get financial compensation. How much you get will totally depend on how serious the allegations were and the seriousness of the harm it caused you. Where a court decides in your favour, it may not be just compensation that you are offered or indeed looking for. At this stage, an order called an injunction may be preferable to stop the publisher of the statements being able to do so again. In an out of court settlement, these would be called undertakings. If successful, the court is likely to order the other party to pay most, if not all, of your legal costs as in the UK, we still follow the principle of "loser pays". A point to bear in mind if you find yourself on the wrong side of the coin.

————

What to do if you receive a cease-and-desist letter?

First of all, as I said before, don't let the emotion overwhelm you and don't respond out of anger. There will be a clear timeframe in which you have to respond set out in the letter, so let it simmer before you speak to anyone because wasting legal costs on telling your lawyer chapter and verse about how you have been treated is nothing more than dead money. We need the facts and nothing more and whilst, as humans, we would love to spend time getting to know you, we just want to do the best job based on the circumstances with the emotion removed. I know that feels harsh but it's in these moments we have to remain objective. It doesn't matter how much we like you or dislike the other party, it won't sway the conclusion we come to as to how you need to respond to the cease and desist but it could end up costing you more in what's already a fragile situation. This is all said with love, by the way.

But what if you are at fault... what should you do then?

The best action you can take at this stage if, when you really dig into the detail you are able to understand why the other person saw your statement as defamatory, is to take a step back, take advice where you feel it's necessary and not react immediately.

The person who has written to you is likely to have asked you to remove the content, undertake not to publish anything like it again and in some circumstances, publish an apology. As we have talked about above, this is entirely a question of judgement on your part and the facts of the particular case. There is still room to negotiate at this stage

----

What can I do about a bad review?

Dealing with reviews can be difficult, especially when they are not positive. Generally, a review that is both truthful and an honest opinion is permissible and therefore unlikely to amount to defamation. I know that is a tough pill to swallow when you feel like you have done everything possible to help someone or do the right thing. In some cases, a response addressing the issues can be seen as an opportunity to show good customer service.

However, if you can prove that the review is not factually correct, you may then have a right of action and the best approach would be to remove the review and tell the reviewer why you have done so. If, despite attempts to remove it, the review remains, then you have the same options that we have spoken about - effectively to weigh up whether or not to send a cease and desist.

What goes in a cease-and-desist letter?

Firstly, lets recap again on what you need to be satisfied with before you send out a cease-and-desist letter. The defamatory statement must meet the following requirements:

- lowers you in the estimation of 'right-thinking' members of society generally,
- disparages you in your business, trade, office, or profession,
- exposes you to hatred, ridicule, or contempt, or
- causes you to be shunned or avoided.

As explained above, a cease and desist is a professional and succinct letter that is often, though not always, enough to stop the offending party and if it doesn't stop them, it is your proof that you tried to resolve the matter amicably. The letter itself will include the following details and it is always advisable to have lawyer draw up the letter for you as if it doesn't meet the criteria set out in the civil procedure rules, then you could have costs awarded against you or even worse you claim be struck out early in proceedings:

- How the statement was published, including dates,
- Why it is defamatory,
- How it is likely to cause harm,
- An instruction to stop or cease posting the statements,
- A threat of the risk of further action,
- Actions or undertakings you want them to provide.

Providing the recipient with a deadline for ceasing the allegedly defamatory action gives more weight to your letter and compels the recipient to react quickly so be sure to do this. The deadline should remain reasonable, for example allowing the recipient 7 or 14 days to respond shows the court should you reach that stage that you acted reasonably.

A copy of, or at least a sample of, the content you believe to be defamatory should also be included in in your letter, or a schedule to it.

Defamation is an extremely emotive subject but by having a basic understanding of the legalities of it will keep you one step ahead of the game and give you some understanding of when to take action, so well done for getting this far! When you are in the thick of these situations, it's so easy to under-estimate how much more difficult it will be to take on board advice.

CHAPTER 6

SHE SAID WHAT?

A GUIDE TO HANDLING COMPLAINTS & CREDIT CONTROL

The biggest part of running any business is dealing with customers and clients. As we talked about earlier in this book, your terms and conditions are an integral part of your onboarding process. It's not all about what happens at the front end of the client or customer relationship however that counts, how you manage the relationship throughout the journey is equally as important for you to avoid complaints and maintain the reputation for excellent customer service that you are striving for.

Inevitably, situations will arise where a customer is not entirely satisfied. It happens to everyone and it's your responsibility as a business owners to really embrace the tough the days. This is when your resolve will truly be tested and you will need to step into that role of CEO. Managing these situations effectively, proactively and without emotion will serve you well! I know it is so much easier said than done, I have talked a few entrepreneurs down from the emotional ledge over my years, but this really is one of the biggest mistakes I see being made when it comes to customer complaints, let that ego go!

You need to keep cool and remember that it is not about you. It's not a personal attack on you, although I know it can definitely feel like it in the moment. It is a criticism of your business, service or product. Now, I know you will be reading this right now and thinking "What on earth is she talking about? Of course, it's about me. It's about my business, my baby, my life's work, my creations..." and I understand all of that, I really do. But this is business, and YOU have to remember that. A complaint is nothing more than a customer or client expressing dissatisfaction in a product or a service they have received - they are not attacking you as a human and the sooner you adopt that stance and can detach yourself from the outcome, the sooner complaint handling will just become another everyday part of your business. Just another process you and your team have to follow through on.

No two entrepreneurs are the same and not all personalities will work well together. Accept that the client's view of your product or service is not a reflection of you or what you stand for. It's not about your values, it's just a complaint, rightly or wrongly, against something happening within your business at that moment in time.

When you don't come from a position of authority, receiving a complaint will send you into a spin and your natural response is likely to be panic, anger or perhaps upset because you will feel personally attacked and that will cloud your judgement and how you respond in the moment. By having a written complaints procedure and working on accepting that this is an inevitable part of business you will be able to respond from a position of clarity. Yes, of course there will be times when unfounded comments or complaints are made about you when perhaps it is more personal but on the whole the reason will be linked to how someones feels about what you have sold to them, rightly or wrongly.

Take a step back and review it from a place of every customer has the right to question a service or product that they feel doesn't meet the standards they expected – yes, I know that's a tough stand point, but it will most definitely help you in these situations. Do you remember we talked about what a reasonable standard was? It's entirely different for every business and industry, so only you will know if you have met the service level expectations you promised. So, take the emotion out of it as far as you can.

———

What do you do when you receive a complaint?

First, look at it from the customers perspective and try to be as objective as possible. Put yourself in their position. How would you be feeling right now in their situation? Generally, speaking as a lawyer, putting yourself in the position of the other side is something we only do to work out our next move, never to empathise because of course, we are there to fight for our clients and too much empathy for the other side would become a hindrance. But, as a business owner, this is something I have really worked on. There are always two sides to every story, and by considering the position from the other persons perspective, a lot of the heat can be taken out of the situation.

Each of our customer's journeys are different and coming at a complaint from their perspective rather than from our own often positions of pride can often lead to a much quicker and more favourable outcome. Understanding should be at the heart of everything we do.

Now that doesn't mean that the customer is always right, I am not saying that at all - that's an outdated perspective and one that savvy customers and clients have grabbed onto for dear life to justify poor behaviour, so don't ever get caught in that trap. Maintain your boundaries but always be open to see a situation from both sides.

The aim of a good complaint's procedure is always to find a resolution, not to start a dispute!

When a customer expresses their initial dissatisfaction with you but it's not yet a formal complaint at, think about how you can make the process simpler and more straightforward for them. The reason I say this is because under consumer legislation (if you are a consumer led business like we discussed in chapter 4 this will most definitely apply to you), we have a duty to make sure that the process is clear and simple. We can be penalised for making complaints or cancellation procedure's too complicated for customers to navigate so keep that in mind. We have all been in those situations where we have tried to cancel or get in touch with a company to discuss a complaint and you are taken through a website with no contact details, a call centre that spans the globe, and then a voicemail box that is probably never going to be accessed, so keep that in mind and keep the process lean.

Direct them to your complaint's procedure, so that they feel heard in the moment. Another benefit of doing this is that it gives both parties space and time to think, and actually takes the immediate emotional charge out of the situation. Be polite, try not to show your frustration and thank them for reaching out to you, thank them for the feedback and confirm that you are now moving them over to your formal complaints procedure which will give them all the information on how the process will be led from this point including, clear timeframes for responses and confirmation of who will be handling the complaint. Remember that it doesn't have to be you, especially if you feel like you will not be able to judge the situation professionally and without emotion. You can pass it to another team member or if you don't have a team, think about using a lawyer; we've handled many complaints on behalf of our clients for this very reason.

Just having that initial bit of 'space' can make such a huge difference in how the complaint will progress. When your customers or clients have to think about actually what they want to say in their complaint, and that it will be reviewed properly, calls for a more focused approach, and one that you can properly respond to. It's so easy to lash out in a message, call or voicemail, but when you take the lead and control the situation by having a clear policy setting out what you need from your customer/client, you can stop the situation becoming more inflamed and emotional than is necessary.

Keep in mind that customer complaints as you grow are inevitable, you will never be able to please everyone but just remember in those moments we have a duty as business owners to objectively assess what you are being told and then use it as feedback to improve your service. Most of these situations happen because there is a break down in communication or because the parties expectations of each other just weren't clear enough when they started working together, something we covered earlier when looking at your terms and conditions, so keep that in mind and always be willing to evolve.

Also try to avoid any unnecessary delay when handling the matter. I know, I know in these situations often you just want to run and hide, but don't. Lean into the difficult parts of business too, they will only serve you and a delay will only cause more distress and frustration.

Approach the situation positively, point them in the direction of your complaints procedure and then follow the procedure to the letter!

————

So, what are the key principles to a good complaint's procedure?

I have learnt over the years, and from working with and for some of the largest and most successful corporations in the UK, that the key principles are:

- Be Honest - being transparent and honest about the truth of the situation will serve you well. There is a saying that you cannot argue with the truth and for the most part, that is true. Once people understand the situation fully, they are much more open to a discussion and when they feel heard and respected, by receiving the truth rather than excuses, a resolution can be found much more quickly.
- Listen - we touched upon this above but really hear what is being said to you.
- Communicate - acknowledge the complaint quickly, if you can, within 2 working days. Tell them how the complaint will be handled and when they can expect to receive a full response so that you can manage expectations and prevent being chased unnecessarily, as that is frustrating for both sides.

- Investigate - check your terms and conditions, speak to everyone involved. Have the deliverables been delivered? Have the expectations been met? Consider all the details before reaching a decision on the outcome of the complaint.

- Respond - When you respond to the complaint, set out what you have investigated and what you have found. Include as much detail as is required to ensure the customer understands how you have reached your conclusion but not too much so as to complicate the situation. Keep your communication respectful and clear and try to avoid being provocative with your language; and

- Learn - Take what you can and learn from every single situation where a client has raised a complaint. Absolute gold can come out of these situations because sometimes we are so heavily involved in the day-to-day running of our businesses that we can fail to see the bigger picture. Taking on feedback in a positive way is not always easy, but it will always improve your product or service and will make you a better leader.

Having a clear and simple complaints procedure, with not too many steps involved, will help you to streamline the process and conclude any issues quickly, so be sure to do this work and set a procedure that will work for you when these inevitable situations arise.

But what happens if the customer isn't happy with my response?

If a customer or client is not happy with the outcome of your investigation, you have the option of allowing them to appeal, where ideally, someone else in your business will review the situation and your previous outcome. Beyond that, there is a risk that the matter could escalate into a legal dispute which is of course, what you should be hoping to avoid in most circumstances.

Should a complaint escalate beyond the internal procedure, at this point it would be advisable to take advice as it is likely that your complainer will be doing the same. Having the right advice early on is key to make sure you don't say something that could impact the outcome of your case.

As we saw with Eva at the beginning of the book, receiving a letter from lawyers can be distressing so don't try and handle that on your own. What a lawyer will do in this scenario is weigh up the risk of, do we give the money back, or do we fight it from a financial and reputational perspective, and give you initial advice so you can be sure of how you will progress and take out the fear of the unknown, as far as they can. If your lawyer believes that your case is weak or even that you have a strong case, but it will cost you more to prove that in court than to pay the refund, I would hope at this stage they will tell you that. Yes, there is a chance that you will recover your costs from the other party if you are successful, but what if they can't afford to pay?

If you take the view that the case is just not worth fighting then there are tactical ways in which your lawyer will approach the case so as not to admit liability and possibly cause damage to your reputation, and it would be advisable at this stage to document this via a settlement agreement so that you have contractual obligations preventing either of you from talking about the situation once matters have been finalised.

But what happens when your client or customer simply doesn't pay and there is no complaint?

Finding yourself in a situation where you have completed a service or provided goods to someone, and they then default on your payment terms can feel very frustrating. Sadly, it's not uncommon and is not always a case of "can't pay" but more like "won't pay". Having customers essentially use you as a creditor in their business is something that all business owners at some point will come up against and collecting cash can become a huge drain on a business owners time if not managed effectively.

Not having a proper handle on your cash collection means without doubt that your business will eventually struggle and when you are juggling that against also trying to preserve your client or customer relationships it can become a serious source of stress.

There are some early steps you can take to limit the risk of debt recovery being needed but of course inevitably at some point you will have to move towards a formal recovery procedure. I'm sure you have had those moments where you have thought it is just not worth the hassle, we all have. It feels like a lot of energy to chase money but if it is money you are owed for work you have completed or goods you have supplied then of course you deserve to be paid properly for it.

So, what can you do upfront to minimise the risk of customers defaulting?

Get paid upfront - this seems so obvious but if you are paid in advance then the risk of you not being paid is removed entirely. It can feel daunting to ask clients or customers to pay in this way, but we wouldn't go into a shop ask for goods and then tell them you will pay them later. This is something that we had to implement in our business and while yes it will mean some people will choose not to work with you it also means that those who do are truly invested in the relationship between you.

Have staged payments - an alternative is to have payments once certain milestones have been reached and a mechanism whereby you don't move onto the next part until payments are made up to date.

Interest for late payment - yes include a term in your contract that if you are not paid on time then you will charge your customer interest.

Have very clear payment terms - any ambiguity in your contract or terms and conditions around the payment terms can confuse customers and leave you exposed to the defence that they didn't understand the contract. Be clear on what is expected with regards to payment.

Communicate well with your clients - this again may seem obvious but having a customer or client who feels able to approach you means that you will be aware of potential risks before they happen and can often find ways around the situation.

Have a robust credit control procedure - this is probably the most important point. Treating all credit control and debt recovery in the same way and having strict procedures that you follow up with will prevent payment delays becoming full on disputes.

In essence the more work you can do early on to limit the potential risk of non or late payment the more beneficial it will be to your business and much less of a drain on your time and resources.

———

What does a good credit control procedure look like?

Credit control will never be a one size fits all but there are some key stages that will alert you to how serious a matter is becoming. I call these Informal, Formal and Active and I will take you through each of those stages so that you can start to identify potential debt recovery situations in your own business. One thing that is for sure is that the better you know your ideal client and/or customer and have an understanding of their behaviours the easier it will be to implement a procedure that fits the needs of your business.

You also need to know your numbers and be up to speed on your finances including when payments are due to you and any amounts outstanding so that you can take fast action. Without knowing and having a way to monitor this basic information it will be impossible to stay on top of cashflow in your business.

Having a term in your client and customer contracts that allows you to charge interest on your late payments can offer a small incentive to pay early and stick to the payment terms and of course threats of litigation can help but they won't always be enough to stop you losing out financially so what are your options? Here's some ideas for you.

Stage 1 - Informal Action

If you think about your creditors right now you will mostly likely be able to identify at least one client or customer that would fall into this category. These are the clients who perhaps have got in touch to say they are struggling to make your payment or who may only just have missed a payment. They could even possibly be someone who is a few payments behind, but you think they are good for it and have a pretty good relationship, so you are happy to work with them for a little while.

While I know the temptation in these situations is to do nothing, don't do nothing! Even when you are trying to work with your clients and preserve the relationship it is really important to instill clear boundaries, even at this stage and managing the situation is critical to make sure your customers don't mistakenly think that a late or missed payment is acceptable to you. Yes of course there will be moments is every businesses lifetime where cashflow can feel tight but it's in these moments that we have to stay in integrity and keep the lines of communication open, running and hiding is just not an option.

In this phase of credit control, I advise my clients to have a suite of debt recovery letters that they use in each and every case. Another standard operating procedure that just becomes part of your business processes. Hopefully by now you would have reached out via telephone email and possibly even text but once it's passed in my opinion 2/3 days of lateness your procedure should be instigated, especially if your customer is not responding.

So, what would you include in these three letters? (And these can be sent by email, if that's how you would usually do business, there is no need for over formality here)

I would suggest something along the lines of;

Day 3 (after due date of payment)

Letter 1 - confirming that the payment was due on x date and that you are sure it's a mistake but that they need to bring the payment up to date within the next 7 business days. Suggest that they get in touch with you if it's likely to be a longer term problem so that you can discuss it in more detail.

If you do not receive communication back and no indication that payment will be made within 7 days, then you should send letter 2.

Day 10

Letter 2 - Acknowledge that the payment remains outstanding and express your disappointment that they have not been in touch to resolve the matter. Take a more formal tone and confirm that you now require payment to be made by the close of business on x date. I would suggest 3 days as reasonable to prompt a response or hopefully payment.

Day 14

Letter 3 - where payment is still not received confirm that the matter is now being considered for escalation as the payment is now 14 days late, and that if you do not receive full payment within 48 hours you will be handing the matter over for formal debt recovery action. At this point you may also want to confirm that interest is now accruing on the debt in line with the terms of your contract.

In most situations this will trigger payment and/or an arrangement for a payment plan to be put in place which should hopefully prevent any further action being necessary. I totally understand that this process can feel uncomfortable, no one wants to be exerting pressure on people who may already be in financial difficulties but equally your business is not there to provide a line of credit to your customers and having clear and proper boundaries that you follow across the board will make this situation easier.

But What happens if they still don't pay?

Then we activate Stage 2 - Formal Action

As we discussed in earlier chapters you cannot issue a claim through the courts unless you have already made reasonable attempts to settle the matter, and this is no different when it comes to debt recovery. If you do not act reasonably, you may find yourself subject to court penalties which are usually financial and could mean that you may not be able to recover all of the money owed to you, which is of course not where you want to be. Having followed a clear stage 1 informal procedure up to this point, will provide some evidence that you have attempted to resolve the issue amicably but it doesn't go quite far enough.

The standards for reasonableness are set out in Pre-Action Protocols contained within the Civil Procedure Rules and it is those rules that the court will look at those to decide if you made a reasonable attempt at settling without their intervention. There is no specific pre-action protocol as such for debt recovery claims but there is general guidance that can be useful.

Having already written to your debtor to chase a few times and no doubt sent another copy of the invoice, perhaps even made some more phones calls now is when the formality should be stepped up so there can be no uncertainty between you that payment is now required as a matter of urgency.

A final letter (Letter before Action) should then be sent including the following information;

1. Set out the full details of your claim
2. Specify the full amount outstanding include interest and potential costs and be clear on what the amounts are for.
3. Allow a further reasonable period for payment.
4. Confirm that court proceedings will follow if payment is not made within the suggested timeframe
5. Mark the letter "urgent" and "final demand"
6. Send a further copy of the original invoice and any other relevant documents, this could include your contract or terms.
7. Once the deadline has passed for payment make

another final attempt at calling your debtor to resolve the issue.

The aim with this whole process is to exert pressure but also show that your debtor has been treated fairly and given a number of opportunities to resolve the issue with you without the need for the courts to use their powers.

Keep a diary of everything that you do including telephone calls and keep a record of all the correspondence that you send and have received from the debtor.

An alternative to the letter before action is a late payment demand. This allows you to claim interest, compensation, and your reasonable debt collection costs under the Late Payment of Commercial Debts (Interest) Act 1998. You can do this provided both parties were acting in the course of business, so this won't apply if you deal solely with consumers but is a useful tool for business customers.

Where an invoice is not paid or is paid late, the Act and Regulations 2002 & 2013 allow you to charge interest at the annual rate of 8% above the base rate for each day your invoices are overdue.

You are also entitled under the same regulations to charge compensation against your debtor if an invoice is overdue by as little as a day. The compensation you are allowed to charge depends on the unpaid debt amount so as you would imagine receiving a formal demand with an increased amount owed and escalating can be a useful tool.

So, what if I still don't get paid?

This is where is starts to get serious. The stage where you are
being forced to consider real legal protocols for recovery of
your money and is what I refer to as an Active stage of debt
recovery.

There is an element of common sense needed here. What I
often see is frustrated business owners sometimes with a dent
in their pride because they are out of pocket and are likely to
either have been ignored by their debtor or ended up in
conflict, refusing to look at the situation from a commercial
perspective. It's where it becomes about winning at all costs.
Don't let that be you. Talking entrepreneurs down from the
metaphorical ledge has become a bit of a pass time for me
because yes, it's tough when things don't work out the way
you planned or you feel disrespected by someone you have
invested so much in. All I can say is remember why you are
in business. It's not because you want to make friends, sure
that's a great by product of nurturing great relationships but,
you are in business to make a profit and throwing good
money after bad is nothing short of stupid. There I said it,
don't take it personally but I have to be clear here fighting
someone who can't afford to pay you before you go to court
won't make them pay you if you go to court. You will just
lose more money.

Now obviously that's not always the case and I am massively
generalising here, but you can be sure if someone has fallen
into financial difficulties and has not paid you despite all of

your threats there is a risk that they just do not have the money.

It doesn't make it fair, but it does make sense that you shouldn't then go all in and spend more money that you are unlikely to get back especially if it's just to prove a point.

There will however be situations where you know someone can afford to pay you, or they have assets that they can call on to pay you and then there are real remedies open to you to resolve the matter.

The first and probably most aggressive tactic for recovery is a Statutory Demand, but what is it?

A statutory demand is a formal written demand for payment of a debt, and it gives the debtor 21 days to make the payment to you. If they do not pay within the 21 days and either fail to apply to have it set aside if they are an individual, or fails to apply to restrain the creditor from presenting a winding-up petition where the debtor is a company, the creditor can use the statutory demand as grounds to present a petition to the court for a bankruptcy order or winding-up order.

The reason why a statutory demand can be used to support petitions for bankruptcy or winding up of a company in this way is because non-payment of a statutory demand within 21 days is deemed to be evidence of the debtor's inability to pay his (or her or its) debts by the courts.

The only restrictions on use of this procedure are, if it is a company that owes you money the debt must exceed £750 and where it is an individual the debt must be greater than £5000.

The other option open to you is issuing a county court claim - but how do you do that?

Essentially there are two ways to start a claim, the first is by issuing a claim through county court money claim centre (CCMCC) and the second, is by making a claim online using MCOL where you will need to register. I have linked to these sites in the resources section at the end of the book.

You can pay the court fees online by credit or debit card. Court fees are usually less when you opt for the online service.

Once your claim has been issued you then have to wait for a response. The best possible outcome is that the defendant does not respond to your claim in time because without their response you can apply to the court for what is referred to as a default judgement. The response is needed within 14 days of the date it is deemed service on the defendant (deemed service usually being two working days after you have issued the claim form) or this can be extended to a further 14 days if the defendant submits to the court a form called an acknowledgement of services within the first 14 days. Are you still with me?

If you obtain default judgement that is an order for payment of your claim in full, plus court fees and interest, and you win by default.

If the defendant does wish to respond they have various options available to them and depending on the option, they choose will determine how the case then progresses. The options available to them include admitting the claim, promising payment, asking for time to pay, or proposing payment by instalments or they can choose to defend the claim and must then provide full details of their defence together with evidence to the court within timeframes laid down by the judge usually by way of directions. Once the courts have all of the information they need to be able to validly assess the claim a date for a final hearing will be scheduled.

Often by the time a case gets to this stage the parties will have legal representation in place and they will handle the formality of the situation on your behalf but sometimes you may choose to attend as what is known as a litigant in person and this means that you will be representing yourself and your evidence to the judge.

If you do decide to go down this road preparation is everything, so make notes of your key points. And rehearse what you intend to say. Make sure you take all of the evidence and records that we spoke about earlier with you and if you feel equipped preparing a chronology of events will also be useful and show the judge that you are well prepared. The hearing is likely to be before a district judge and will usually be quite informal, don't be put off by the dramatic scenes we see on TV, however it is always wise to dress smartly. This is still a formal court setting and as much as I would like to tell you that the pomp and ceremony is no more, I'm afraid I can't so you just need to play the game and respect the institution.

The debtor should also attend court or send a lawyer to represent him. If no one attends, your case will be much simpler, but you should be prepared for the possibility of your matter being adjourned to another date.

You will present your case. Essentially, this is just going through your particulars of claim, explaining the detail. The judge may ask you questions, and you can refer back to your paperwork if you feel the need before responding. Sometimes the pressure of being in a court setting can feel overwhelming but try to stay composed and remember you are all just human beings.

The other side will then get a chance to present their defence and go through the same process, try not to interrupt but do makes notes of the points you disagree with so you can raise those if you get the opportunity later, the judge is likely to ask you if you have anything further to add before coming to his conclusion.

Once you have done that, the district judge will decide the case. He should explain his decision and tell you what order he is going to make. That order will be typed up by the court staff and it will then be posted out to both parties.

If you win the court will order that you debt, be paid and you will also be able to claim for the court fee you have paid, plus some reasonable costs.

If you lose, it is unlikely you will have to pay costs to the debtor, but you may have to pay his travelling expenses and maybe loss of earnings of up to £90.

Of course, going to court and even winning doesn't always guarantee payment but the process is designed to protect you in these situations and there is a post claim process that can help you with enforcement if the debtor still doesn't pay.

CHAPTER 7

STOP WORKING ON GOODWILL

HOW TO COLLABORATE AND WORK WITH OTHER BUSINESSES SAFELY.

I f I looked you straight in the eyes and asked how often you work or have worked on goodwill alone with another business owner, what would your honest answer be?

I bet I can take a punt at it being more often than when you have actually put a proper written contract in place, and most definitely more often than I would like you to. Now that may sound patronising, its really not meant to, you're an intelligent business owner and as I have said before there really is no judgement here. I can only share with you the truthful outcomes I have witnessed over the last 20 years in the legal industry and I promise that acting on goodwill alone very rarely ends well.

I totally get why it happens. Business happens quickly and some days you literally can feel l like you are flying by the seat of your pants. You want to lean into your intuition and do what feels in alignment in the moment but an agreement without negotiated terms and thoughtful consideration for the whole process breeds nothing but uncertainty and frustration.

I see you, you just want to get your product or service to market but, even the most basic of written agreements can provide you with enough detail to prevent a long and expensive legal battle, so why wouldn't you?

Ive heard the all the reasons; the relationship you have won't end in a dispute, you're friends, you respect each, you would never "go legal" on each other... but I have also, many, many times, been the lawyer being instructed because it has all gone wrong and witnessed the upset and hurt it can cause, we're only human right? Dispute's aren't uncommon, they can, and unless you are extremely lucky, will happen at some point in your business journey if you don't put the right protections in place.

It makes total sense for you to collaborate and join forces with another incredible business owner there is power in two or more that we can rarely replicate as one, but without a proper contract what is that worth? So, whether you are planning a long-term business relationship or a one-off project, there are some contract fundamentals that I would suggest you consider before taking the leap.

It's also really important for you to think through your collaboration terms before you start selling because, whether it's written or not, you are forming a legally binding relationship and only a fool would leave those terms to chance. On the flip side, you also have clients who will be contracting to work with you so even if you don't see your collaboration as worthy of a proper contract, they most definitely will.

What is it going to look like from the client's perspective? Who are they contracting with? Is it one of you or both of you? Is it your company or you personally? Who has the liability if something goes wrong?

These are all points that need to be discussed as early as possible and ideally and drawn up in a proper legal contract giving protection to both you and your business partner and also your prospective clients.

I love seeing business owners collaborate and watching the magic that happens when two brands align, especially in the online world. It can be a lonely space, sat at your desk, day in, day out, on your own, so it's no surprise that a collaborations can feel so alluring, but you have to protect yourself and your clients.

A key point for instance, when you collaborate with another freelancer or business, is that new intellectual property is being created. It's a new joint idea, a joint creation, new content and you need to be clear on how that intellectual property will be owned. If we don't think about these things at the beginning then when you get to the end of the project there are way too many questions left unanswered that can leave you exposed to risk.

Great collaborations come from an open and collaborative mindset and you cannot achieve that without exploring the detail. Working through the minutia at the beginning, keeps the communication flowing, you're talking and learning more and more about each other and your long term goals and aspirations, you're thinking about the best outcomes for both of you, not just about the best outcome for you. Coming at this negotiation with a powerful, professional persona of a CEO who sees the true value in working with others and the need for protection for all will make your collaboration even more than you ever expected it to be.

Expectation can be so damaging if the details aren't explored. How can you possibly know what someone is expecting from you and from a business collaboration if it isn't thrashed out?

———

But, let's start at the beginning, what actually is a collaboration?

A collaboration (also sometimes referred to as a joint venture) is an agreement between two parties to co-operate in some way. The relationship should be document through a collaboration or joint venture agreement that sets out the arrangements between the parties. A collaboration is an alternative to two or more parties setting up a new entity such as a limited company to go into business together, instead they operate under a contractual arrangement.

There are many reasons why this type of contractual relationship is preferred over setting up a new company such as less administration, wishing to retain control over your assets or because the relationship is not intended to be permanent plus it can be more beneficial from a tax perspective (subject to individual accountancy advice on the particular project). But thats not to say that there aren't also benefits of also setting up a completely new and separate legal entity so consider all of your options before you go ahead.

———

What should I be thinking about before we enter into a formal collaboration agreement?

Well, let's think this through strategically, why are you doing this and how do you want it to work. Ask yourselves and discuss what is the main purpose of the collaboration? Is it for a one-off project? What's the commercial objective - profit? exposure? audience building? Will the project run indefinitely or for a certain period or perhaps until you have reached a certain goal? Don't be afraid to explore all of these factors.

Another important consideration is to think about how long you are willing to negotiate for? Its helpful to have a date in mind that if you have not managed to finalise the terms you are contracting under that you will stop, you're busy and having ongoing negotiations left open for month on end can become a drain so be clear on when you would like to have an agreement in place by.

Also think about how you will protect the confidentiality of the ideas you are discussing. A non-disclosure agreement (NDA), sometimes also referred to as a confidentiality agreement is a contract that secures the commitment of the parties to protect the confidential nature of the new business ideas you're coming up with. This stuff is important, right?

It's easy to skip past these parts to find only a few months down the line, that the person you had your discussions with are either going ahead with the project themselves or even worse collaborating with another party, with all of your ideas. Frustrating? Yes. Immoral and lacking in integrity? Probably. Illegal? NO. If you do not preserve the value of your ideas then you are very much at risk if you discuss those ideas with someone else so while an NDA may feel like overkill at the time, I promise you, it's a powerful tool in any entrepreneur's toolkit. You will undoubtedly feel like you are suggesting the person you are speaking to is dishonest but as with any other part of business don't let your mindset hold you back. Any savvy and commercially minded business owner knows the value of pushing through those insecurities and just focusing on the outcome. Asking people to sign an NDA should become another standard operating procedure in your business, when it becomes just another process it will feel so much easier to approach.

The legal position when signing in an NDA is pretty straight forward. The person disclosing information receives a contractual promise from the person they have disclosed information to that they will not share that information with a third party. Sometimes additional clauses can be added into the NDA to permit disclosure to certain third parties but on the whole you would be contracting not to share the information at all. The aim is to protect important and commercially sensitive information and there are a few things to consider when putting an NDA in place.

The first thing to think about is why you are sharing the information in the first place, for the purposes of this chapter it is likely to be because you have an idea that you want to approach another business owner with, with a view to entering into a collaboration but it could also be with a supplier or potential client. An NDA can cover a multitude of situations. The purpose should be clearly set out in the NDA to make sure the information can only be used for that very specific purpose by the person you are sharing the information with.

Other things to consider include a clear definition of what information you are disclosing. What is the confidential information you are sharing, be as specific as possible here as in the event of a breach you need to be able to prove what was protected information.

It might sound obvious but also be clear on who you are disclosing information to and from what date. Anything said before the date of the NDA would not automatically be covered so make sure you have your document signed as early as possible in the discussions or explicit terms setting out everything that is confidential that has been discussed. When it comes to the parties to the NDA you need to be very clear on who you are authorising to use the information. The wider this definition the harder it is to monitor the information sharing so keep this as clear as possible.

At the most basic of levels a recipient of confidential information needs to keep that information safe secure and confidential. Sometimes additional provisions can also be drafted in where there are additional requirements for record keeping or cyber security but the level of protection you need will comes down to your individual circumstances and the sensitivity of the information.

The importance of an NDA and need for attention to detail when drafting one should not be underestimated because a properly drafted and well written NDA will give you a sound contractual right that in the event of a breach you can bring legal proceedings against the other party which is much easier than trying to take a claim to court for a potential breach of confidence action - something I will not elaborate on for the purposes of this book. The aim is to keep you out of court!

So, once you have your NDA and have considered other metrics you would like to work to, detailed negotiations can open up on your new collaboration.

———

So…what terms should you be discussing? Let's skip to the good bit…

This is where the magic starts to happen..

When working out the terms of a collaboration you can never have too much detail. Discuss it all. The more detail you go into in the beginning the better and start to get those ideas down on paper. Really iron out the detail of the project from beginning to end but also look at the bigger picture, like I mentioned above what's the aim or the outcome that you are hoping for, will it be a one-off project or something you are looking to build on to potentially sell on? By having this overview of the whole project and its purpose the finer detail becomes much easier to discuss because if you get stuck on a point of negotiation go back to the reason for the project and if that particular issue doesn't move you forwards to the end goal, then scrap it and move on. As entrepreneurs we have a tendency to move in different directions but sticking to a clear strategy with the end goal in mind will serve you well, the applies of course to when you are collaborating or day to day as an entrepreneur.

Once you have agreed on the project and are ready to move forward and collaborate then you need to put it in writing! There it is again. There are many reasons why an agreement is necessary but the most important is to formally document the project and set out the parties' respective obligations and responsibilities.

There is no legal obligation to put a collaboration agreement in place, they are nothing more than a private commercial agreement between you and another, but you would be ill advised to collaborate without a formal agreement in place. By putting a legally binding contract in place you ensure that the risks you are taking are calculated and managed and in the event that something does not go as planned that you have a right of recourse - a contractual right which as we have said before is much easier to take action against.

What if I don't want a formal agreement?

I hear this a lot. "A contract isn't aligned with how I run my business" or "I feel it makes our relationship too serious or scary" As I said at the beginning of the chapter I get it, I know it's important for your work to feel aligned and that intuition plays a part in the decisions you make but I also know the importance of having a proper written agreement, whatever industry or sector you work in. The risks associated with not having a proper agreement go far beyond just falling out with a business friend. The first thing to consider is that even where there is not a proper written agreement a contract is still being formed. A verbal agreement between two or more parties is still a contract but what comes with that with a verbal agreement there is much less certainty on the terms you have specifically agreed and in the event of a dispute arising makes it much more difficult for a court to interpret and you could find yourselves in the hands of a judge who is deciding what you intended. Another factor to consider is if your project needs financing or insuring (which is should) then a funder or insurer will most certainly want to see a proper agreement being put in place.

If you find yourself in the mindset of not wanting to implement a proper legal agreement when collaborating, ask yourself why? Is it because you are not really sure of the project, in which case you shouldn't be doing it? Is it because you are worried you may not be able to commit? Again, think it through is this the right thing for you right now? Don't ever enter into a legal relationship with another business owner unless you are willing to go all in. You owe it to each other and the clients you will be working for or with. Hopefully it will simply be because the legal side of business can sometimes feel overwhelming but that's simple enough to work through because the more you dive into it the easier it will become. Just another standard operating procedure.. Another reason I sometimes hear from people when they don't properly document a contractual relationship is because of cost. I say this with love but that will never be a good enough reason because your financial risk without proper terms is so much greater.

———

So, what should you be including in your agreement?

First of all lets think about the type of agreement you may want, if you intend to collaborate on many different projects with another business owner it may be that you use something referred to as a framework agreement where you set out terms that allow you to work on multiple or successive projects without needing to have a new agreement for each project. A framework agreement will often include provisions confirming how the detail of the future projects will be agreed ie through a statement of work on a project by project basis. Of course the detail of the individual projects may differ but the more general terms can be set out and agreed as general framework. Alternatively you may have a one off project where all the terms you agree between you will be thrashed out at the same time and included in that one agreement, either way can work well and simply depends on if the collaboration will run on and possibly into many projects together or if it will be a one off.

There are some really key terms that you should include in your agreement for it to be properly fit for purpose and these may include;

Purpose and the detail of the project - this can be included in the beginning of your agreement or often it is set out in a detailed schedule at the end. This part of the agreement should include the resources needed for the project, the contributions of each party and the expectations of each throughout the life of the project. Are you each going to carry out a specific part of the project or will you work jointly throughout. It is also worth considering your marketing plan, if its clear include it in your agreement. You can never have enough detail here and a brief overview won't ever be enough. The aim is to try to avoid having to revisit the terms later in the project. Some flexibility of course will always be needed as there will always be moving parts to any project that need tweaking once you have started but on the whole iron out what you can, as early as possible.

Whether your agreement will cover the day to day operational elements in detail is up to you or you can choose to keep that less formal.

Duration of the project - the term of the collaboration may be for a fixed period, or it can be ongoing. Either way that needs to be documented to ensure expectations are going to be met and both parties are available for the whole duration. Whatever you decide, try to include key dates for deliverables and a project timeline so that you can accurately measure performance. It may seem formal, but it will prevent a lot of frustration because keys dates are being missed or deadlines are too vague.

Exclusivity, confidentiality and permitted use - much like with your NDA you need to follow through with the confidentiality provisions in your collaboration agreement to ensure that you are both still clear on what information you can and cannot share outside of the project and set limits on how the information you share about your respective businesses can be used, especially if it is commercially sensitive. Remember you will be sharing data and you need to have clear guidelines of what's expected of each other. Another important consideration is whether the relationship is to be exclusive to each other or are you free to also contract and collaborate with other parties?

Reporting and how the project will be managed day to day - the key to any good collaboration is strong communication between the parties. Whilst it is not essential it is useful to set out reporting requirements that fit the needs of your project. These don't need to be detailed unless your particular project calls for it but having clear guidelines and expectations on how matters will be reported will be invaluable to keep a good flow of communication between you and avoid conflict.

Finance and funding your collaboration - key provisions around funding are paramount to the success of the collaboration and being clear on how much each party has to contribute and when, will make for a smooth partnership. Think through how your project will be funded? Consider if you will need to set up a new business account to collect payments? If not, who will be invoicing your new clients and customers and how will payments between you be dealt with? What if you need to raise more capital? What are the expected costs? As with any business idea having a handle on finance and cashflow is absolutely imperative to its success. Also e sure to include a provision confirming that each party s to be responsible for its own taxes. Don't be afraid of the unknown, by working through these ideas early on it forces you to consider the pitfalls and risks of the project and foresee any potential problems. It may be that one of you are bringing the ideas and the other is financing the project. Left to chance and proving this arrangement to a court in the event of a dispute can be really difficult so protect yourselves and put down as much detail as possible.

Intellectual Property - depending on the nature of your project you will also need to consider including provisions to protect your individual intellectual property rights meaning those you are bringing to the collaboration together with any new Intellectual Property that will be created by the collaboration. This is referred to as foreground and background intellectual property. New foreground intellectual property is created when you come together to create a new project. This could be the name of your project, the copy included in your joint content, the systems you create as a partnership - none of this existed before you came together, and you will want to discuss how that new intellectual property can be used at the end of the project. For instance, are you allowed to use the content again in your own business or can you use the name of your project when not working with each other. All of that new Intellectual Property has goodwill attached to it, so it is essential that you are clear on how any profits made off the back of that goodwill are to be distributed during and after the collaboration. Will one of you retain ownership of the new Intellectual Property and licence its use to the other or will it be owned jointly for instance. When you came to the project there is likely to have been Intellectual Property in your existing business which was appealing to your collaborator, it is likely to be one of the reasons you were drawn to each other. You will want to make sure that any of the Intellectual Property you brought to the project remains in your exclusive ownership and is only licensed to the collaboration for that specific purpose.

Other keys terms will include limitation of liability and what representations and warranties both parties are relying on when entering into the collaboration.

Having a well drafted, comprehensive collaboration agreement for your new venture may seem like overkill when you first start out but without one your investment, even if that is just your time, could be at substantial risk so push through those barriers. When that little voice in your head starts telling you it's not necessary, or you'll be fine because you are mates just remind yourself this is business and every single part of your business and your time within it deserves total protection.

Chapter 8

Team Building

The big freelancer or employee debate.

As your business grows, you can very quickly feel like you are becoming stretched beyond your resources. Often, client work is booked out, and trying to fit in all of the things that you need to do to grow your business can feel really overwhelming and it's at this point in time, that you will probably start to feel like you are being pushed way beyond your limits. It's then at that point sadly for most of us that we start to think taking the plunge and passing over some responsibilities to someone else.

Entrepreneurs by their very nature have a drive and need to be in control of every element in their business especially in the early days and that combined with perhaps limited finances in the beginning can mean that building a team is left often too late. Passing over responsibility to another can be a difficult decision to make but outsourcing the parts that are not where you are needed even if you enjoy them can make all the difference. If we really think about it, you wouldn't see Sir Richard Branson or Lord Alan Sugar desperately trying to spin all the plates, and they certainly wouldn't be where they are today if they did.

First of all, it's ok to feel nervous. Why wouldn't you? You have probably spent years by now growing your client list, perfecting your offers to make sure your clients get the best service from you and perfecting your brand, not to mention all the hours you have put into making sure your audience get to know, like and trust you, so it's not at all surprising that you wouldn't want to let the reigns go. The risk that another person can bring to your business is real and getting the right fit is imperative to this relationship and the next stage in your business being a success, so give yourself a break and plan the steps you need to take.

If you are reading this chapter and this is a way off for you right now, then just flag the section and be sure to come back to it before you decide to go all in. If you are coming back to this chapter, you are probably now considering venturing into the world of outsourcing or employing (or may already be there and just want to check you've done it right), so well done on getting this far - your business is about to hit a whole new level.

The next stage in your business is a natural progression. It's not because you're not good enough to do it all or aren't organised enough or are rubbish at technology, it's simply because that's what happens in business; it grows, right! We hear all the stories of entrepreneurs getting to 7 figures while sat on a beach, sipping a mojito, and never having needed support and yes, that may be true for the odd person, but I can assure you, it is not the norm. You will need support, and I'll say it again, we don't see any big corporate CEO's juggling social media, accounting, IT, legal, HR, marketing… do we? As the saying goes, "there is no I in team", but be sure to choose that team wisely.

The rewards that come from starting to see parts of your business moving to the next level without input from you, and tasks being ticked off the "to do" list without you having to do all the work and all the hours are incredible. For me it was when I really started to feel like I was running a "proper business." It felt so liberating not be shackled to the parts of my business that I knew I had no skill in.

I have worked closely over the years with many leaders and their human resources teams to support them on employment law matters and what I have learnt through doing that, and from employing 4 full time staff and 2 part-timers myself, has given me some really valuable insights and steps that you too can implement when working out what that support in your business looks like.

First, I would suggest you write down a list of the tasks that you feel the role needs, so everything that you will expect this person to do. Once you have done that you will have a clearer view on whether it is a general assistant role that you need or a very specific service. When the service is clear, for instance, if you want someone just to run your social media accounts, outsourcing to a third party is much more straightforward as you will find most freelancers (not all, of course) niche into one specific area, so the decision is simpler. A more general role may need you to do more searching to find the right fit. It is not impossible, but it can take a little more time.

The process of being absolutely clear on the tasks included in the role also helps you to write a clear and concise job description because applicants, or people pitching you for the work, need to be clear on exactly what the expectations of that role are. This is one of the key issues I see when disputes happen - that the expectations weren't set out properly at the start.

I would then suggest you write out a list of specific attributes for the type of person you are looking for and have two columns - essentials and preferred - listing the attributes that fall into each. For instance, must have a law degree, must have experience of [list your preferred] accounting system, must have grown a successful social media account, would like them to have more than 3 years' experience, would like them to have worked previously in an online business, would like them to understand [relevant] coaching techniques. Be as specific as you like here, there are some things we can teach as employers or contractors about our businesses but if you are counting on this person picking up the gaps that you don't currently have expertise in then you need to be sure they can fill the role 100% and anyone who doesn't have all of the non-negotiable's should be disregarded on the first round of considering the potential applicants/contractors.

It sounds brutal, right? But this is one of the biggest mistakes I see entrepreneurs make; sometimes because we like a person, or get a good feel for them, it can cloud our judgement and while someone may be able to grow into a role, you just haven't got time for that at this stage of your business. Once you have an established team it is much easier to rely on intuition or make a judgement call and I am totally behind that, but when you have a specific need and are feeling nervous about expanding your business, whether that's through employing or outsourcing, then the fit has to be right. A bad experience at this stage will have an impact on future decision making in this area so don't risk that.

Another good tip is to have an application form instead of using CV's when recruiting employees and design the form with questions that directly link in with the needs of the role. Quite often a CV will be far too generic, and you will have to do quite a bit of work to figure out if they have everything you need. A questionnaire or application process will immediately highlight any gaps between the candidate and the role.

So do your due diligence and prepare upfront, and hopefully, the right people will come to you. With freelancers, speak to others who have had an experience of them, look at their testimonials, ask them to show you examples of their previous work - the right people will be completely happy to oblige and make you feel at ease… and once you have all of this information, making the decision is much easier.

As with anything, preparation is key, but intuition will also play a part and if something is screaming no at you, pay attention to it. Our first instincts are far too easy to ignore but will stand us in good stead if we use them wisely.

It doesn't all come down to you and your business, however. In today's market, attracting and retaining good staff can be a challenge as good talent will be highly sought after. When they are deciding who they want to build a career with, research is showing us that more onus than ever is being put on work life balance, how much flexibility a role can offer, company ethics and future progression. To able to attract the right calibre of candidate as a business owner you need to know your brand, have given thought to the future of your business and be able to demonstrate a clear understanding of the role you have to offer.

We have also seen a huge shift in working patterns and practices, in more recent times due to the pandemic, however over the last decade flexibility has become a buzz word within the employment industry and something employers are being forced to consider seriously. With many more people now working remotely the line between employees and freelancers, it could be argued, has become even more blurred so when you are recruiting, it's important to be absolutely clear on the employment status they you are engaging your people on (for instance, employee or freelancers and so on) as this will have an impact on the employment rights they acquire, how much tax they will pay and who makes national insurance, and pension contributions.

Employment tribunals and HM Revenue & Customs may not always follow the definition you attach to an employment relationship and may take into consideration different factors when they are deciding on an individual's employment status which may mean that someone you work flexibly with under what you deem to be a freelance arrangement may be able to prove employee status for the purpose of employment rights.

So, what is an Employee?

Under The Employment Rights Act 1996 an employee is defined as an "individual who has entered into or works under a contract of employment" A contract of employment is then defined under the Act as a contract for service and this could include an apprenticeship whether it is made orally or win writing or implied into a relationship.

What rights do employees gain?

There are some essential characteristics that an employment relationship must have if they are to be classed as an employee. For instance, they need to be engaged to perform work personally, not through a company (subject to IR35 rules), that you as the employer have a duty to provide them with work and you also have control over when, how, and where they do that work.

Directors and shareholders of a business or partners in an LLP can also be classed as employees if they work for the business.

Having status as an employee is significant because employees gain employment rights. Some rights, such as the right to have the tax and national insurance paid by their employer and the right to receive pension contributions are acquired immediately. Other rights will be acquired over time, such as the right to claim unfair dismissal. Since 6 April 2012, employees have to work for a continuous period of two years before they acquire full employment rights, which is referred to as the qualifying or two-year rule. Prior to 2012 this was one year.

This list summarises the main rights that an employee has;

To receive a written statement of terms and conditions on the day they start work.

To statutory sick pay

A right to continuity of employment when a business is transferred (defined as a transfer of undertaking).

A right to maternity, paternity, adoption, and shared parental leave and pay.

A right to time off to care for dependants.

The right to a minimum notice period.

Protection against unfair dismissal (this is subject to the two-year rule)

When requested to have a written reason for dismissal

The right to equality of treatment if on a fixed term contract to those who are permanent (subject to some caveats)

Redundancy rights and statutory redundancy pay

The right to request flexibility of working after the first six months of continuous service.

So, what is a worker?

This is where the employed/self-employed relationship starts to get a little more blurred and care needs to be taken when defining those who work for you. The Employment Rights Act 1996 confirms a worker as a worker if he or she entered into or works under a contract of employment or some other contract and does work or provides services personally to another party who is not their client or customer. This definition is much broader than that of an employee and under it all employees are workers but not all workers are employees. For instance, some freelancers will work under a "contract for services" and could be determined as workers as opposed to purely self-employed.

So why is all of this important I'm sure you're asking yourself? Workers will also acquire some employment rights so unless that is your intention then you need to be sure you are putting in place very clear unambiguous terms and that your behaviour reflects those terms. There are three key matters that are taken into account when considering if an individual is in fact a worker and these are, is there a contract? Are they obliged to provide services personally? And do they work for others so are they in business on their own account?

If someone who works for you is then deemed a "worker" under these rules they would acquire the following employment rights (for clarity these rights also apply to employees);

A right to paid annual leave

A right to breaks

The right to receive the national minimum wage

Equality of pay

A right not to be discriminated against

A right to be accompanied to disciplinary & grievance hearings

Health and safety protections

Trade union rights

Equality of treatment between part-time and full-time workers

You can see from the list above that it is essential that you are contracting with people in the right way if you wish to avoid necessary employment rights attaching to their service and genuinely operate under an arm's length contractor relationship the way to do this is with proper terms setting out specific rights as a freelancer or contractor that they will benefit from.

So, what makes for a genuine Freelancer or contractor relationship?

It may seem basic but one of the most important factors here is the right of the individual to "substitute" someone else to do the work that you are engaging them to do. Why, you might be thinking? Well, because having the right to substitute someone else into their business to cover their contract in times where perhaps they won't be available, on holiday, unwell or just on another contract evidences the independent nature of the relationship and the lack of control of one party over another.

When you engage people on a contractual or consultancy basis, they have very few employment protection rights and of course are taxed differently. Genuine independent contractors run their own businesses and the contracts they are therefore engaging with you on are at their very heart commercial.

As your business grows and you start to think about ways to lessen the load on you, outsourcing to a freelancer where you get the benefit of support without the commitment of taking on an employee, is a great way to start to build your team but, getting the terms of that relationship wrong or not understanding the true nature of a genuine contractor relationship could result in you being in deeper than you ever expected to be.

To avoid the risks here there are some key things to consider when taking on a self-employed contractor such as - they should be quoting you for the work rather than you setting a fee, they will not work under your direct supervision and will generally govern how when where and for whom they work for on any day, they will submit invoices for payment of work that has been completed, they will pay their own tax and national insurance and may be VAT registered so you could be subject to a charge for VAT on their invoices, they won't have holiday pay as we said above they should have the option in their contract to substitute another and have their own staff or associates where necessary to help them to do the work in their absence (this can be subject to your agreement on the person who will be working for/with you but this should be included in your contract).

It's really important for you to be clear and understand which factors make someone employed or self-employed before you start working together because getting this wrong can turn into a very expensive problem later on.

There's lots of individual factors for you to take into consideration but on the whole the main factors that would be looked at if the relationship was ever in question would be;

- No mutuality of obligation – this means that the

self-employed are not guaranteed any work and do
not need to accept the work that you offer them.

- Right of substitution – a self-employed individual
  can send along another person to carry out their
  work.

- Control – self-employed individuals can control
  when, where and how they carry out the work
  whereas an employee is provided with hours of
  work and is told what to do.

- Financial risk - self-employed staff are often paid by
  the job or project and they can make a profit if they
  complete the job quickly or lose money if the
  project overruns or has to be reworked. They will
  have their own insurance to protect themselves from
  errors or accidents.

- Working for other clients – it is expected that self-
  employed freelancers will work with different clients
  or perhaps be engaged for short term projects. Your
  freelancer may become an employee if they have
  worked regular hours for you over a period of time.
  After two years they will gain full employment rights
  such as the right to claim unfair dismissal.

So how do I prevent an issue down the line or a dispute with
my contractor?

Talking to your freelancer and exploring all of the details of
the arrangement before they start working for you will clarify
the expectations of both parties. If you are on the same page

and both agree that the relationship will be one of self-employment document it, PUT IT IN WRITING and then make it clear that they need to be registered with HMRC as self-employed and will be responsible for their own contributions. Also, be clear that they are not an employee and therefore will not have certain employment rights such as payment for sickness, holiday, pension, and maternity provisions and that the arrangement is not permanent and can be ended at any time (subject of course to whatever you agree in your contract).

So, what is an agency worker?

An agency contract allows a temporary worker to come into your business, but they are engaged by an agency, not directly for you. You enter into a commercial services contract with the agency to provide you with workers on a temporary basis and they engage their own contractors who they then pass over to you to complete your work. It is the agency who finds the individual the work who is responsible for paying them and you do not have any direct responsibility for payment to the worker.

This can be a really useful way to dip a toe into the world of team building but it's not without risk. A key point to note is that anyone that works over 12 weeks for you will have the same employment rights as an employee, therefore it is imperative that you make sure your contracts remain of a shorter term if you want to avoid the employee/employer relationship. being inferred into that relationship.

I work with volunteers - what do I need to think about when I do this?

Volunteers are a great way to build support into your business and help other gain valuable experience in your industry. They are unpaid save for being allowed to reclaim genuine expenses but sometimes when your volunteer is doing a great job you may feel called to pay them a little extra. Don't do it. Now I'm not being mean by saying that it's a great thing to do at a human level but as we have said earlier in the chapter every worker is entitled to receive the UK's national minimum wage and if the sum you pay happens to fall below that – your gesture of goodwill could find you in a situation where you are at risk of a claim.

Yes, the law can get a little crazy like that but regulation is there for a reason and good intention won't always be enough to avoid liability. The reason for this is because when you make a payment an employer/employee relationship as opposed to that of business and volunteer could be inferred into the relationship and your volunteer could then be acquiring important employment rights, so keep it simple.

Let's take a closer look at discrimination!

Engaging people to work with and for you requires some thought as we have considered above. Employment legislation and protecting the rights of individuals is an important area and it is no different when it comes to the rules surrounding discrimination. This is not a subject you can take lightly, nor should you want to, in any area of your business. Promoting diversity in the workplace is integral to good people management. It centres around valuing everyone as an individual but to truly meet the standards of an inclusive society and see the benefits you need to create an environment where everyone feels able to participate and aim for their full potential irrespective of individual characteristics.

UK Legislation and in particular the Equality Act 2010 goes some way in setting minimum standards expected within the workplace and throughout working practices however this in unlikely to go far enough in ensuring the right protections and behaviours are being demonstrated by businesses. Best practice in this area would be for you to have a diversity and inclusion strategy that goes beyond meeting minimum standards, one that actively promotes employee wellbeing and diversity across all groups of people whether that be age, disability, gender, race, sexual orientation, religion and gender identity and reassignments. These are referred to as protected characteristics.

Another area where employers can be left at risk of criticism relating to discrimination, but one that isn't publicised to the extent perhaps it should be, is during the recruitment process. Even at this early stage in a business relationship an employer has duties to uphold against potential employment candidates.

Discrimination as defined under the Equality Act refers to the less favourable treatment of individuals because of a protected characteristic (as set out above).

Discrimination however is not always direct and obvious and when it comes to the recruitment process you need to be careful so as not to place a condition on the role that could potentially discriminate against a group of people, for instance this is commonly done when a role is cited to be full time and you're not willing to consider any other options. Sadly, women are still classed as or believed to be a sector who do the dominant share of the childcare therefore by placing a condition on a role that it needs to be full time can exclude women so be open to the role being a mix and don't be so rigid in your advertising so as to exclude groups or individuals.

You should also bear in mind the requirement to make reasonable adjustments at an interview stage for those with disabilities. It would be wise to ask your applicants if they require reasonable adjustments to be made if they are called for an interview. Reasonable adjustments can include physical changes to the place where your hold your interview, it could also include adjustments to assessment times or consideration of whether an interview needs to be held in another format or with translation. I know as a business owner especially when you are up against it trying to recruit that all of this added pressure can feel overwhelming, but an accusation of discrimination will feel much worse. What is reasonable in the circumstances will depend on the facts of the particular case. Question yourself when considering these matters and if it feels unreasonable or a little off it probably is and if you are ever unsure just take advice. It is much better than having to take advice down the line because a claim has been issued against you!

Other factors to think about include when drafting a job description, carefully consider the genuine requirements for the role. Does it need to be full time, or could it be done in a more flexible way for instance through a job share? Take care also with advertisements to avoid any potential discrimination especially when using ads targeted at specific groups for example as this could cause issues if you relied on something that's a protected characteristic for instance somebody's age or sexual orientation from receiving the information.

When you are deciding on candidate selection be sure to draw up a shortlist based on the requirements of the job that you've already detailed.

At the interview stage then be sure to keep a thorough record of what was said, and the responses given. Under data protection legislation a candidate who has not been offered a role can request a copy of the information you hold on them to be able to assess why they were refused for the role so do bear all of that in mind.

Another important point to note relates to when you are making an offer of employment to a candidate. Be sure to make it "subject to contract" and subject to certain conditions being met. In the UK we are now required to ensure that our team members are eligible to work in the UK so this is a question that you should be asking your potential new employees to provide evidence of. Other conditions you may want to include are; proof of qualifications held or references being supplied.

Once all of the conditions have been met your offer of employment would become unconditional and the employee is then open to accept the offer. Remember also that requirement we considered earlier that the employee should receive a written statement of terms or even better their employment contract on the first day that they start working with you - this was previously within 8 weeks, but it is now on the start date of employment so don't get caught out with that. That's not to say you are being policed and this fact will be checked but a disgruntled employee and their lawyers in the future in the event of a dispute or claim arising would look at all of this finer detail and try to find fault so be prepared.

When inducting your staff, a great starting point is to talk them through the whole business, of course you have to give them the basic information on health and safety and the job specific requirements, but the bigger picture is important too. Talk them through your products or services, tell them about your suppliers, discuss your brand values and future goals for the business - what's the five-year plan? The more information an employee has about the business as a whole, research suggests, the more invested they become in its future. Feeling part of whole as opposed to just the small part they may be playing makes your team feel valued, listen to their thoughts and opinions and always be open to taking on board peer review. Critique should come up the chain as well as going down so don't be afraid to hear from your employees on what's working well and what's not going so well, it's an opportunity to improve.

Some other important factors to consider when you are building your team and bringing on senior members of staff who will undoubtedly have access confidential and fundamental information about your business is the use of restrictive covenants, also sometimes referred to as restraint to trade clauses. The courts are not particularly fond of unfair provisions seeking to restrain the trade or profession of an individual but providing the terms you include in your contracts are fair and just they are an acceptable mechanism to reduce the risk of commercially sensitive information about your business being used inappropriately.

Cases that have come through the courts and looked at what would be considered reasonable and unreasonable in these circumstances, and there is a general view that narrow geographical restrictions and an average length of 12 months as a restricted period would be deemed reasonable, however it will always come down to the facts of your particular case so always take advice when drafting provisions such as these. You can be sure that a restriction preventing someone from working anywhere in the UK for any industry for a period of 24 months would be perceived as unreasonable so take care and weigh up the commercial benefits of the restriction only imposing restrictions to properly preserve your business, not to act as a penalty because an employee chooses to move on.

This is particularly difficult for online businesses as quite often you're marketing and working across a much bigger geographical span but trying to restrict a person from working with any other online business in your industry or sector is unlikely to be upheld by the court.

Restrictive covenants can relate to not using company information, not taking clients of the business, not trying to set up in competition with you, not stealing you staff or using your suppliers but the overriding principle here is that they are there to protect legitimate business interests and not for any other purpose or they could be perceived an unreasonable if the facts are questioned.

Ending an employment relationship can feel heavy, right?

It doesn't need to. It's all about being prepared and having the right information. In the most simplistic of terms unless you are dealing with a case of gross misconduct employees are always entitled to receive proper notice when they are being asked to leave their job.

The minimum statutory entitlement is one week for every year of service up to a maximum of 12 weeks. If, however in your contract you have contractually bound yourself to a different period of notice (and this would only ever be greater than the statutory minimum, not less) then that is the period you should follow.

If you do not give an employee proper notice required under their employment contract you could find your side subject to a claim for wrongful dismissal.

Unfair dismissal claims are a hot topic. We often hear employers referring to the two-year rule and that there is no risk of a claim against you from a disgruntled employee within that period if you behave badly as an employer when dismissing someone, but this is not entirely true. If the dismissal can be linked to some areas of discrimination or the dismissal is linked to an employee whistle blowing, then you could still find yourself subject to a claim so do bear that in mind and take advice if you are ever unsure. Other claims for wrongful dismissal, unlawful deductions from wages and civil claims for breach of contract are all still open to you within the first two years of service.

So, what is an unfair dismissal?

In its most basic of definitions unfair dismissal is where you as the employer terminates an employee's contract without a fair reason to do so or had a fair reason and failed to follow a fair procedure. Procedure is everything when it comes to dismissals, and I would advise that even within the first two years of a person's employment that you use the a fair procedure for any capability or disciplinary matters to ensure all continuity across your business and to create a good company culture.

Also, using a probationary period for new employees is also very sensible. I would usually draft into our contracts a 3/6/9, sometimes a 12-month probationary period as an additional layer of protection because it gives both parties an opportunity to see if they are the right fit for each other. Now you might say that after you have done all of that work upfront you should pretty much have the perfect employee, but I think we can all agree that even with the best will in the world personality clashes can and will happen and while you can plan for so much not everything will go the way you want it to so give yourself the best chance and the right protections. It is much more straight forward to end a contract in this period for instance with just one week's notice. You will find that even within a few weeks that you have got a feel for whether the employee is able to deliver on the promises they made, or you could find that they have poor timekeeping, or aren't able to work within your team.

From a legal perspective when someone is subject to probation, they do not acquire all of the contractual benefits of a permanent employee so for instance they may not have access to a pension until they pass probation or as I said above, they aren't subject to the minimum notice periods.

What they will acquire though is protection from wrongful dismissal so be sure to follow whatever process is set out in your contract and always act fairly, while the probationary mechanism is there to protect employer's tribunal judges don't take kindly to rogue employers who don't follow a fair procedure or their contractual terms. An employee will also have all the usual protections from harassment and discrimination that we talked about earlier so do keep this in mind.

Employment law is vast and yes, the repercussions can be severe but don't let that put you off building your team. With the right support and information, you can make sure you are protected, it's a learning curve but as with everything in this book all about laying the right foundations from the beginning and starting as you mean to go on.

CHAPTER 9

YOU'VE MADE IT THROUGH

How was it? That's an honest question by the way, I would love to hear your feedback.

When I was writing this book, I had many moments where I sat and wondered if I was doing the "right thing". You know those moments as business owners where you just think is this what people really need. The truth is we all have doubt and insecurities sometimes worrying whether what we offer is of true value to our clients, right?

This book was never going to ignite a new business passion in you, inspire you to change your life or directly help you to make a million but it will make your journey safer. Law is never going to be fun or exciting and I know that doing this work can feel uncomfortable and serious and sometimes I worry about that but its when I hear those thoughts coming in that I have to remind myself that your protection and safety is the sexy work for me. Helping you to achieve your goals in a way that makes them sustainable, lower in risk and give you more confidence as result is exciting to me!

That is why I do what I do, not because I think the law is "interesting" yes there are some parts that I love and I will never apologise for the geek in me who enjoys constructing a contract that gets you results and achieves your outcomes, but its more than that. It's about you finding your power and not dimming your light because you are fearful or unsure about where you stand. It's about you being able to be the best business owner or entrepreneur that you can be knowing that you are protected and safe. For me it's always about protection and safety, never about the law.

A lawyer's relationship with a CEO is one of the top five relationships of their lifetime, only next to family and best friends and there is a reason for that. We get to share the good times as your business expands and evolves; we get the calls late at night when you can't sleep because that issue on your mind just won't go away. We are there through the peaks and troughs because law isn't a one-off exercise when you are running your business, it is there every single step of the way and I hope that this book has shed some light on how it can be there to serve and protect, it's not just about limiting or regulating you - it's about opening opportunities and securing your future success without fear.

Whatever the reason you started out on your journey as an entrepreneur I can tell you with no uncertainty that it is one of the most inspiring, bravest, and challenging decisions that you will ever make. Stepping outside of what's perceived as normal and taking a risk in business is not something to be taken lightly. If you are anything like me, I am sure you want to look back on your life and know that you gave it everything you've got, that you gave it every chance of success because you deserve it, every tiny little bit of it. And, as much as business is a risk it is also one of the most exciting and enjoyable rides you can go on and we shouldn't forget that, yes, some parts of it, like this part are more serious but business should be enjoyable, you are designing a life on your terms so remind yourself of that every now and again.

Opportunities to evolve, grow and scale are everywhere - take them! Calculated risks and conscious decision making will keep you moving forward so always back yourself. It's all within you.

My wish is that this book will provide some comfort, guidance, and love along the way, even if at some times it felt overwhelming. I believe that access to legal services should be simple, unassuming, and nurturing. Yes, on times using the law needs strength of character and for you to dive into difficult conversations best foot forward but for the most part it is here to support and guide you through the life of your business.

If there is one consistent piece of advice I can offer it is that everything you do will carry some element of risk in life or business, everything is a choice and in those sliding doors moments don't hold back. Yes, sometimes we can get it wrong, but every mistake is a lesson and an opportunity for growth. Your role is to cultivate that risk and use it to your advantage so by having the knowledge and understanding of the parts of your business that could leave you exposed, you will gain valuable insights into where you can minimise your exposure to that risk. Experience is everything.

So, I hope you've found this useful, I am so grateful that your here and can't wait to see what's next for you but for now cover yourself, PUT IT ALL IN WRITING, breathe in the knowledge and step into being the CEO you know is within you. Don't shy away from the tougher conversations, embrace the complicated parts and be willing to learn, grow and evolve as the leader you are meant to be, I've got you. Playing small because of fear is a waste of you, a waste of your passion and brilliant mind and it will never get you to your dreams. Be fearless, think strategically and remember to always back yourself.

Law and legal protection really doesn't need to be this big scary thing!

With love,

Jo x

About the Author

Joanne Fisher is a business lawyer specialising in legal and brand protection for high earning, female entrepreneurs, and the founder of Get Legal Online™

It doesn't matter where we're from, or how we started or even what we've been through, we all have the right to have it all and to feel safe and protected while we have it. To never feel like we need to fight for our own security.

Her mission is, to pathe the way for women to stop feeling like they're always fighting to get back up, and to stop feeling a need to prove themselves repeatedly. We don't need to take a back seat and let others shine.

We can have all that we want.

We can be all we ever wanted to be.

We can be more.

We may need to push through obstacles and barriers to make that happen, but when we feel supported, protected, and heard that no longer feels as scary, or intimidating.

She's been there, seen it, and lived it. Having fought to prove herself as a lawyer in the corporate world for 20 years, never really fitting in and being forced into a box that just wasn't her. Since leaving that world she's met and worked with so many incredible entrepreneurs who feel those same feelings and hold themselves back because they've been pushed down in the past.

The community of female entrepreneurs online inspires her every single day. Helping women to harness and share their talent fulfils her like the corporate world never could.

Because when you have the right processes, contracts and documents you will feel ready to put yourself out there. Ready to push through the fear and create the life you want, setting you up for success like never before.

When you feel safe and protected, anything is possible.

———

I would love to support you to make sure you have that legal and brand protection in place, for more information on how we can work together visit www.joannefisherlaw.co.uk

For information on my signature programme Get Legal Online https://joannefisherlaw.co.uk/get-legal-online/

Join my FREE Facebook community

https://www.facebook.com/groups/legaltalkwithjoanne

To discuss 1-1 consultancy email

hello@joannefisherlaw.co.uk

Follow me

[f] facebook.com/joannefisherlaw

[o] instagram.com/joannefisherlaw

References & Resources

Resources section of Website:
https://joannefisherlaw.co.uk/links/

Other useful links and resources
Intellectual Property Office:
https://www.gov.uk/government/organisations/intellectual-property-office

Companies House:
https://www.gov.uk/government/organisations/companies-house

HMRC:
https://www.gov.uk/government/organisations/hm-revenue-customs

Charity Commission:

https://www.gov.uk/government/organisations/charity-commission

Charity Commission guidance "CC3: The Essential Trustee": https://www.gov.uk/government/publications/the-essential-trustee-what-you-need-to-know-cc3/the-essential-trustee-what-you-need-to-know-what-you-need-to-do

Consumer Rights Act 2015: https://www.legislation.gov.uk/ukpga/2015/15/contents/enacted

Consumer Contracts (information and cancellation and additional charges) Regulations 2013: https://www.legislation.gov.uk/uksi/2013/3134/contents/made

Sale of goods act 1979: https://www.legislation.gov.uk/ukpga/1979/54

Supply of goods and services act 1982: https://www.legislation.gov.uk/ukpga/1982/29

The Electronic Commerce Regulations: https://www.legislation.gov.uk/uksi/2002/2013/contents/made

Unfair Contract Terms 1977:
https://www.legislation.gov.uk/ukpga/1977/50

Defamation Act 2013:
https://www.legislation.gov.uk/ukpga/2013/26/
contents/enacted

Employment Rights:
https://www.legislation.gov.uk/ukpga/1996/18/contents

National Minimum Wage:
https://www.gov.uk/national-minimum-wage-rates

Equality Act 2010:
https://www.legislation.gov.uk/ukpga/2010/15/contents

Eligibility to work in the UK:
https://www.gov.uk/check-job-applicant-right-to-work

IR35:
https://www.gov.uk/guidance/understanding-off-payroll-
working-ir35

Civil Procedure Rules:
https://www.justice.gov.uk/courts/procedure-rules/
civil/rules

Pre Action Protocols:
https://www.justice.gov.uk/courts/procedure-rules/
civil/protocol

Money claim online:
https://www.moneyclaim.gov.uk/web/mcol/welcome

County Court Money Claim Centre:
https://www.find-court-tribunal.service.gov.uk/courts/
county-court-money-claims-centre-ccmcc

General Product Safety Regulations 2005: https://www.
legislation.gov.uk/uksi/2005/1803/contents/made

Consumer Protection from Unfair Practices Regulations
2008: https://www.legislation.gov.uk/uksi/2008/1277/
contents/made

The Consumer Rights (Payment Surcharge) Regulations
2012: https://www.legislation.gov.uk/uksi/2012/3110/
contents/made

Business Protection from Misleading Marketing Regulations
2008: https://www.legislation.gov.uk/uksi/2008/1276/
contents/made

General Data Protection Regulation ("GDPR"), Data
Protection Act 2018 ("DPA"):

https://www.local.gov.uk/sites/default/files/documents/
The%2BGeneral%2BProtection%2BData%2BRegulation%
2B%28GDPR%29%2B-%2BGuidance%
2Bfor%2BMembers.pdf

Privacy and Electronic Communications Regulations 2003
("PECR"):
https://www.legislation.gov.uk/uksi/2003/2426/
contents/made

Consumer Protection Act 1987:
https://www.legislation.gov.uk/ukpga/1987/43/contents

Provision of Services Regulations 2009:
https://www.legislation.gov.uk/ukdsi/2009/
9780111486276/contents

Consumer Credit Act 1974:
https://www.legislation.gov.uk/ukpga/1974/39/contents

Section 75 rules:
https://www.legislation.gov.uk/ukpga/1974/39/section/75

The Misrepresentation Act 1967:
https://www.legislation.gov.uk/ukpga/1967/7

Unfair Terms in Consumer Contracts Regulations 1999
(UTCCR):

https://www.legislation.gov.uk/uksi/1999/2083/
contents/made

Printed in Great Britain
by Amazon

82290768R00119